CW01658657

THE STORY OF NEWBURY

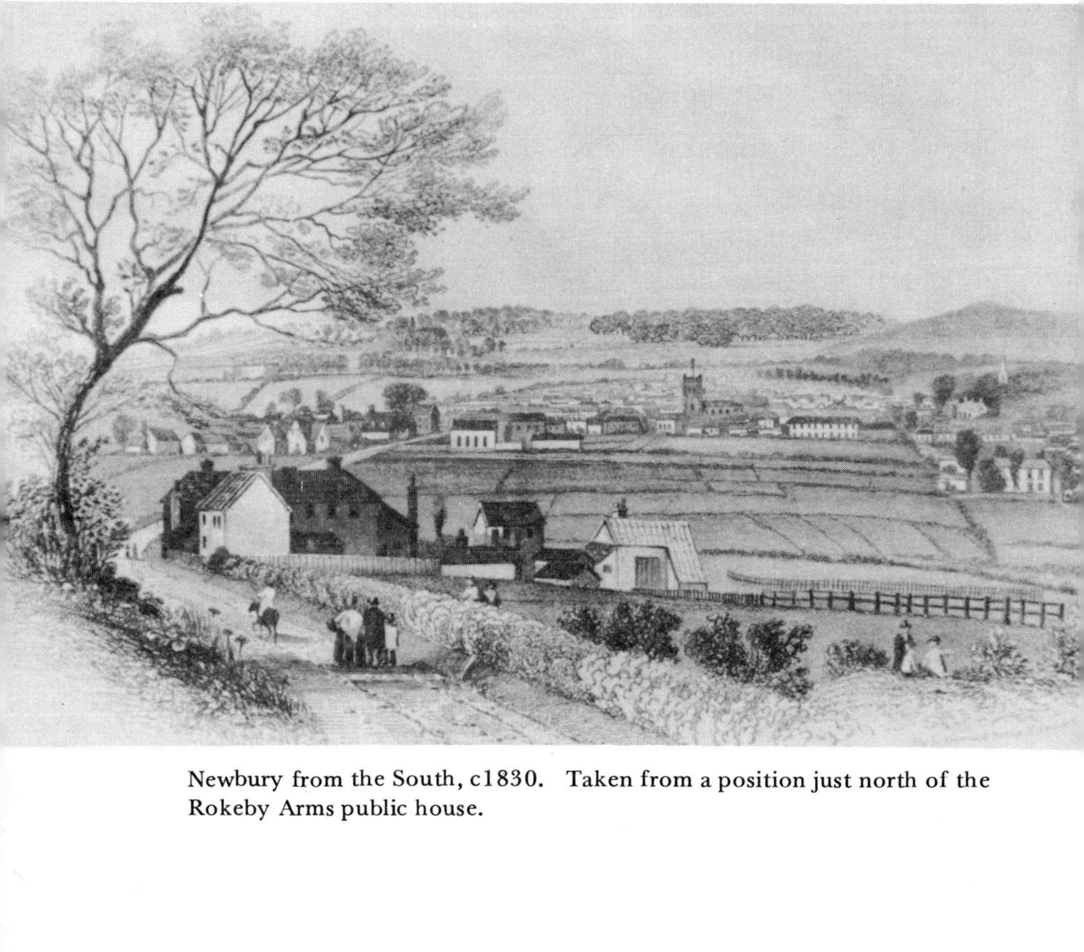

Newbury from the South, c1830. Taken from a position just north of the Rokeby Arms public house.

THE STORY OF NEWBURY

R. NEVILLE HADCOCK
D. LIT., F.S.A., F.R.HIST.S.

COUNTRYSIDE
BOOKS
NEWBURY BERKSHIRE

FIRST PUBLISHED 1979

COUNTRYSIDE BOOKS
3 Catherine Road
Newbury Berkshire

ISBN 0 905392 04 3

Designed by Mon Mohan

Printed in England by Maund and Irvine Limited, Tring, Herts.

Contents

Introduction	9
Municipal History	11
The Locality	14
The Early History	17
The Middle Ages	22
The Late Middle Ages and the Cloth Trade	29
The Civil War	37
1660 - 1800	44
The Nineteenth Century	51
The Twentieth Century	57
The Architectural Heritage	66
Index	93

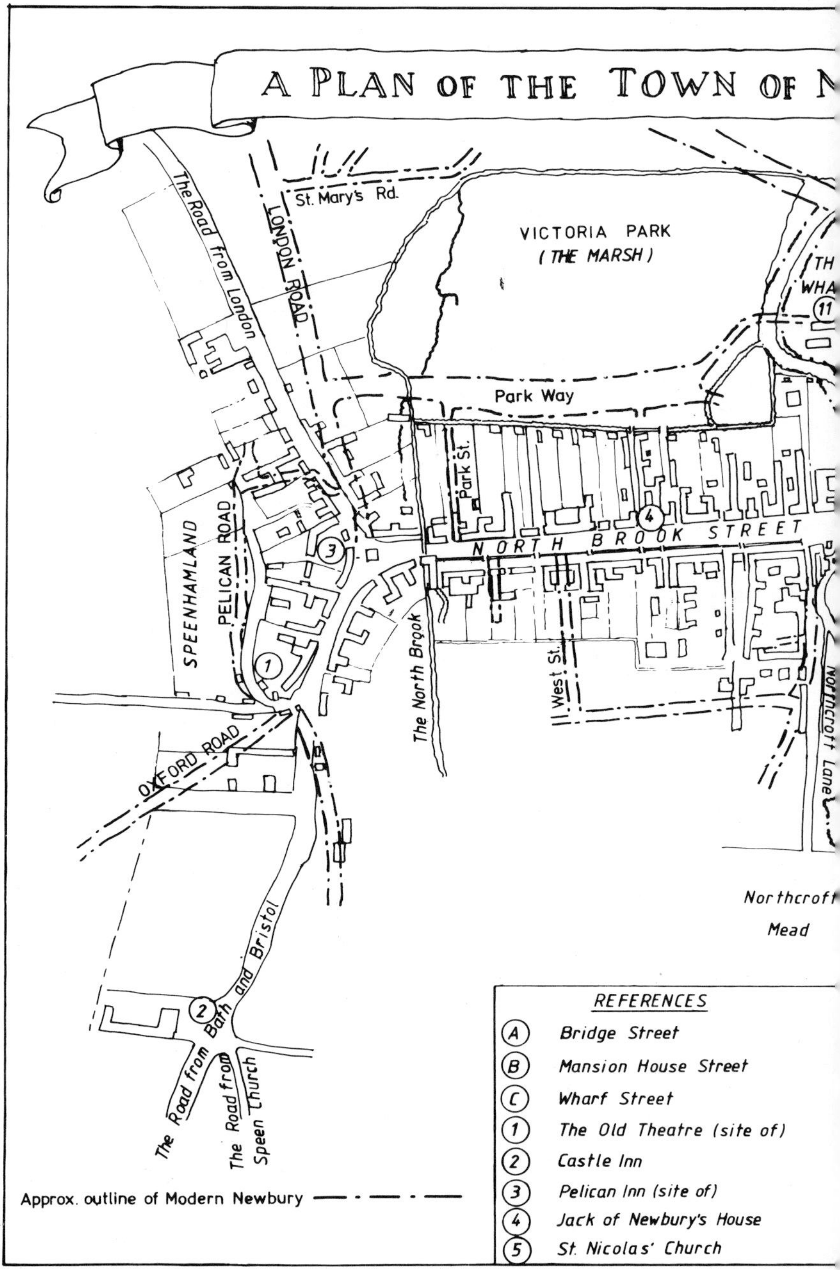

A PLAN OF THE TOWN OF N
St. Mary's Rd.
The Road from London
LONDON ROAD
VICTORIA PARK
(THE MARSH)
TH
WHA
11
Park Way
Park St.
4
NORTH BROOK STREET
3
SPEENHAMLAND
PELICAN ROAD
1
The North Brook
West St.
Northcroft Lane
OXFORD ROAD
Northcroft
Mead
The Road from Bath and Bristol
2
The Road from
The Road from Speen Church
Approx. outline of Modern Newbury
REFERENCES
A Bridge Street
B Mansion House Street
C Wharf Street
1 The Old Theatre (site of)
2 Castle Inn
3 Pelican Inn (site of)
4 Jack of Newbury's House
5 St. Nicolas' Church

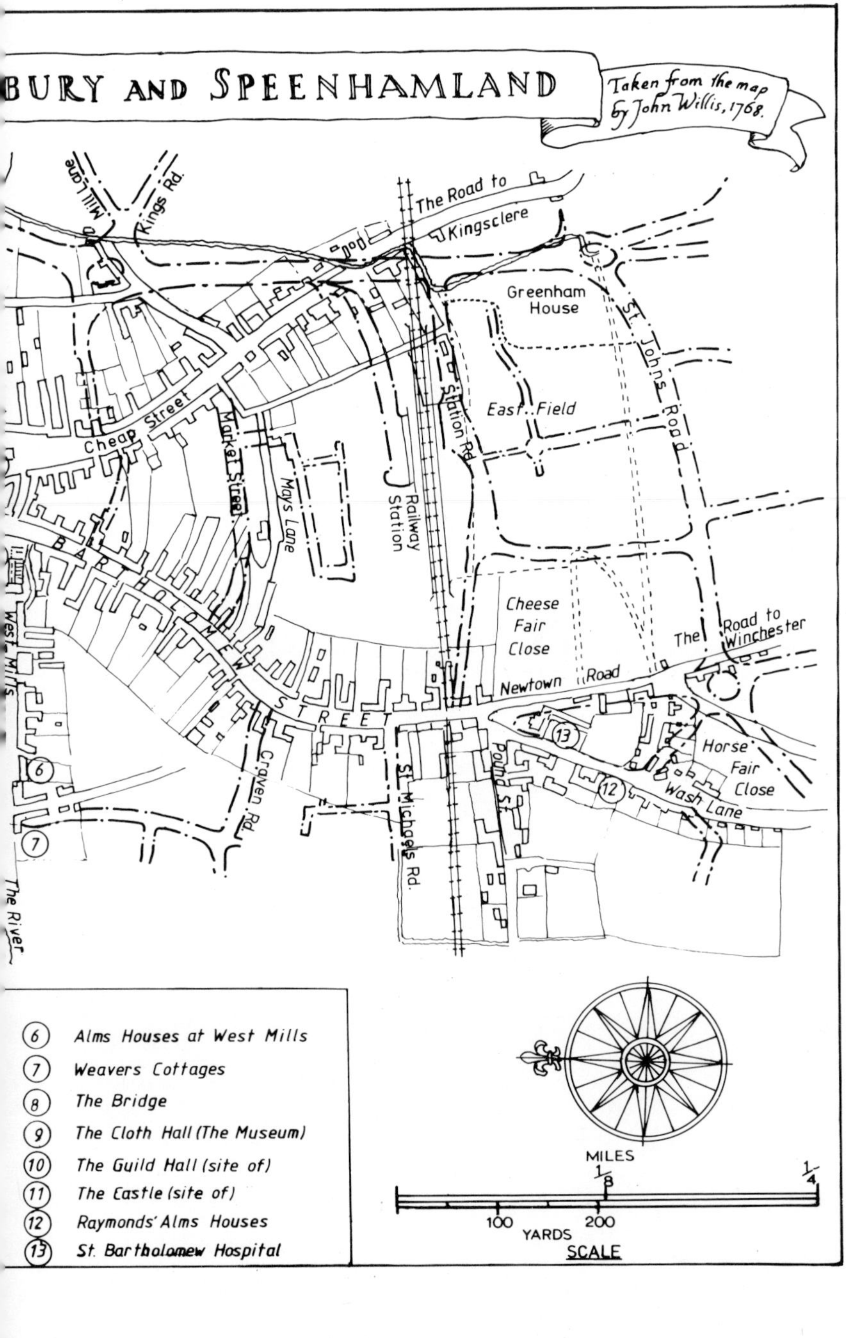
BURY AND SPEENHAMLAND
Taken from the map by John Willis, 1768.
Mill Lane
Kings Rd.
The Road to Kingsclere
Greenham House
St. Johns Road
East Field
Station Rd.
Railway Station
Cheap Street
Market Street
Mays Lane
BARTHOLOMEW STREET
West Mills
Cheese Fair Close
The Road to Winchester
Newtown Road
Horse Fair Close
Wash Lane
Pound St.
St. Michaels Rd.
Craven Rd.
The River
6 Alms Houses at West Mills
7 Weavers Cottages
8 The Bridge
9 The Cloth Hall (The Museum)
10 The Guild Hall (site of)
11 The Castle (site of)
12 Raymonds' Alms Houses
13 St. Bartholomew Hospital
MILES
1/8
1/4
100
200
YARDS
SCALE

Acknowledgements

The Story of Newbury is based on the text written by R. Neville Hadcock, and several local scholars, for the Newbury Borough Guide which was published before the local government changes of the early 1970's. It has now been expanded and brought completely up-to-date with the help of Cecilia Millson and Nicholas Battle.

The photographs of modern Newbury, and that of Jack of Newbury's brass from St. Nicolas' Church, have all been taken specially for the book by E. C. Paine, Ltd. of Newbury.

The Newbury Museum has supplied those illustrations relating to the historical development of the town.

The photographs of Newbury taken at the turn of the century come from the collection of Mrs. Sue Hopson.

The map, based on the town plan of John Willis, 1768, has been redrawn by Max Breach from a copy supplied by the Newbury Museum.

The new District Coat of Arms is reproduced by kind permission of Newbury District Council.

To all the above, and many others who have given invaluable help and encouragement, the publishers would like to record their appreciation and thanks.

Newbury: Introduction

NEWBURY is situated on the River Kennet, a tributary of the Thames, and lies halfway between London and Bath, at the crossing of the main routes from east to west, and from the midlands to the south coast.

The town forms a natural centre for the delightful countryside of West Berkshire and North Hampshire, with varied scenery afforded by river valleys, woodlands, high commons and the chalk downs.

The River Kennet, with St. Nicolas Church.

The centre of the town is about 250 feet above sea level, rising to 412 feet on Wash Common.

There are interesting geological features in the locality; an extensive peat bed in the vicinity of the river, and elsewhere gravel subsoil with beds of London clay. The chalk, from which the region receives its pure and abundant water supply, lies not far from the surface in several parts of the town.

The M4 passes to the north of Newbury, and the Western Region station is on the main line from Paddington to Penzance, fast trains reaching London in one hour, and Plymouth in four hours. The Alder Valley Traction Co. Ltd., and other bus companies link the surrounding villages and long distance coaches from the midlands to the south coast halt in Newbury.

Set in the heart of the country, yet within easy reach of London and the south coast, this is a favoured residential area and popular with commuters. In the midst of rapid development, the town retains an individual charm, typified in its fine main street with handsome buildings, the old bridge giving glimpses of river and canal, and groupings of ancient tiled roofs. Newbury has a strong family atmosphere, and is a healthy and happy spot in which to live and work. It has long been the social focus and shopping centre for a large country neighbourhood, and has two colourful weekly markets. Present day stores offer the best possible selection of goods, combined with personal service.

Newbury is truly a "home town" to those who live in it, and not a holiday resort, yet its fine position, within easy reach of many of the most beautiful and interesting places in England, makes it a good centre for the sportsman or tourist.

Municipal History

The corporate life of Newbury progressed when Queen Elizabeth I granted the Charter of 1596. This ordained government of the town by a Council consisting of 31 burgesses, which included the Mayor and six aldermen. There were to be five companies for the principal trades.

These were :–

Tanners: including barbers and surgeons
Mercers: including all provision dealers and apothecaries
Clothiers (Tailors): including scriveners and schoolmasters
Weavers or clothmakers
Braziers: including builders

Revocations and renewals of the Charter were made by Charles I, Charles II, and James II. There was then little change to the Borough status until 1974 when local government re-organization took place throughout the country as a result of the 1972 Local Government Act. The ancient Borough of Newbury then ceased to exist and its powers were conferred upon the Newbury District Council, a newly created local government body responsible for administering the affairs of a wide area of Berkshire.

The twelve councillors who represent the Town wards on the District Council act as the Charter Trustees and care for the old borough charters and the town insignia. They may elect one of their number to be Town Mayor and another to be Deputy Town Mayor.

The Coats of Arms

The old Borough armorial bearings were granted by the authority of the Earl Marshal of England in 1948. Before that date, unofficial arms depicting Newbury Castle had been used. The Coat of Arms of the former Borough is illustrated on the left, overpage.

The motto was 'Floruit Floreat' – As it has flourished, so may it

flourish. The charges were chosen to depict the cloth trade (teazle) and corn trade (garbs), from which the town derived its early prosperity. A 'bar wavy azure' stood for the river Kennet, crossed swords for the two Battles of Newbury, and the old Castle was commemorated in the crest.

New armorial bearings were authorised to Newbury District Council and these are illustrated above right. They were designed with the wider area of Berkshire in mind.

On the shield itself, four bandlets interlaced at the centre – rather in the way of thread weaving – have been placed. These allude to the Cloth Trade and Newbury's part in it, not least the possibility that the first factory in England was established by Jack of Newbury in the town. At the upper and lower part of the shield a combined charge consisting of a garb and a cog wheel refers to local industries and occupations; the garb to agriculture and the cog wheel to the numerous engineering works in the district including the large government establishments.

Above the shield, the Helm is that appropriate to a corporation: steel visor closed and facing the viewers left. On top of the Helm the Crest itself is in three parts. Firstly, a grassy mount refers to the Downs, then a turreted wall refers to municipal government, and finally above everything is a Cavalier holding a sword aloft to commemorate the two battles of Newbury. The motto is 'Forward Together'.

The Locality

The countryside of West Berkshire, South Oxfordshire, North Hampshire and East Wiltshire, of which Newbury forms the hub, can offer every kind of natural scenery except the sea coast, and even that is within easy reach of the motorist. The walker, cyclist, or driver who is content to explore nearer home, can choose open downland, riverside scenery, woodlands, heath, or picturesque villages. The district is exceptionally rewarding to botanists, as well as to bird watchers, archaeologists and historians.

Around the outskirts of the town public footpaths lead to Donnington Castle, and thence to Snelsmore Common, and to Speen with its Wishing Well, or past the Tudor mansion of Shaw House, now used as a school. South of the river there are attractive walks to Enborne, which has a Norman church and a very ancient bell, and through Hamstead Park. From Wash Common one can walk across meadows to Sandleford Priory, and on to Peckmoor, the remaining part of Greenham Common; or across Newtown Common to Horris Hill. The canal, too, offers peaceful walks away from the traffic, between Thatcham to the east and Kintbury to the west.

A few miles south, off the A34, lies the Sandham Memorial Chapel at Burghclere. This contains the murals which constitute Sir Stanley Spencer's major work, and is now National Trust property. A little further along the same road is Beacon Hill, a landmark capped by ancient earthworks, and the burial place of the fifth Earl of Carnarvon, who excavated Tutankhamen's tomb in the Valley of the Kings, and expressed a wish to rest on the top of this hill overlooking his home, Highclere Castle. Wonderful views can be had from this range of downs, especially above Kingsclere, where King John had a favourite hunting lodge, and from Inkpen Beacon. Near the latter is the highest chalk hill in the south of England; 975 feet. An ancient trackway follows this ridge, from Inkpen to Three Legged

Cross, while north of Newbury the Ridgeway extends across the Berkshire Downs for many miles.

The Lambourn valley is a fisherman's paradise, and contains delightful thatched cottages. Farther north lies the Vale of White Horse where the visitor can explore Wayland Smith's Cave, Uffington Castle, stand in the eye of the horse which is England's oldest hill-figure, or try his lungs at the "Blowing Stone", reputedly audible for five miles. A picturesque ride soon brings the cyclist or motorist to the River Thames via Bucklebury and Yattendon villages. At Pangbourne and Streatley boats can be hired, or the regular summer river steamers may be boarded at any lock for a quiet cruise. Aldworth village boasts a church full of extraordinary effigies of the De la Beche family of "Giants".

Places within easy reach include Savernake Forest, a favourite picnic spot; Marlborough; Silchester, where the Roman wall can still be seen; Stonehenge and Avebury. Littlecote Manor and the Vyne are attractive Elizabethan houses open to the public.

For those using public transport, the small villages can be reached by a network of country buses. Larger centres are connected by a frequent service to Reading, Oxford, Swindon, Basingstoke, Andover and Salisbury. During the summer local companies arrange half-day and whole-day excursions to the sea, and to places of interest, and in winter regular theatre expeditions to Oxford. Main line trains reach Paddington in an hour and Plymouth in four hours, and this time has been shortened further with the introduction of high speed trains.

An excellent general survey of the district about twenty miles around Newbury can be had from Bartholomew's half-inch map "Salisbury Plain", and walkers will need the Ordnance Survey sheets 174 and SU 46/56 for footpaths. Berkshire is not very well served by guide-books, but the newcomer will find the following of interest:—

B.F.W.I. *Old Berkshire Village Book 1979.*

Beckinsale, R.P. *Companion into Berkshire.* Methuen *1951.*

Betjeman, John and John Piper. *Architectural Guide to Berkshire.* Murray.

Channer, Nick. *Berkshire Rambles 1979.*

Chapman, Roy. *Walks Around the Downs 1976.*

Garlick, V. M. *Jack of Newbury 1975.*

Garlick, V. M. *Newbury Scrapbook 1970.*
Mee, Arthur. *Berkshire* (King's England series). Hodder, *1965.*
Millson, Cecilia. *Tales of Old Berkshire 1977.*
Money, Walter. *History of the ancient town and borough of Newbury, 1887. Popular history of Newbury, 1905.*
Money, Walter. *History of Newbury* (reprint *1972*);
Money, Walter. *First and Second Battles of Newbury and the Siege of Donnington Castle, 1874.*
Newbury Museum. *Newbury Buildings, Past and Present 1973.*
Pevsner, N. *Berkshire* (Buildings of England). Penguin *1966.*
Roberts, C. *And so to Bath, 1942.*
Vincent, J.E., illustrations by F. L. Griggs. *Highways and Byways in Berkshire.* Macmillan, *1919.*
Yarrow, Ian. *Berkshire.* R. Hale Ltd., *1952.*

There is much of interest so that the above notes can only be regarded as suggestions. For further information about any of the places mentioned, and others, please enquire at the Public Library. Similarly, the Library should be able to make available those of the books listed above that are now out of print.

The Early History

Palaeolithic Age *(Before c. 10,000 B.C.)*

The Prehistoric History has largely been based upon the researches and writings of the late Mr. Harold Peake, and is of unusual interest. In early prehistoric times the district was almost entirely related to the neighbouring chalk, which were areas of primary settlement. To the north and south of Newbury we find wide expanses of open chalk lands, and it was here that the first inhabitants of the district, men of the Palaeolithic or Old Stone Age, lived by hunting and food collecting.

Mesolithic Age *(Before c. 2,500 B.C.)*

It is difficult to tell when what we now know as Newbury first became inhabited; during the Mesolithic Period (Middle Stone Age), the Kennet Valley must have been a broad marsh covered with swamp growth and impassable to man. At about 4,500 B.C. as the result of land elevation, the river level gradually dropped, the river became narrower and swifter and eventually cut down its bed to some 10 feet below its present level. During these changes the valley floor altered in character, a series of dams and lakes formed, and silting up caused gravel banks and peat bogs to form. Mr. Peake has attributed the dams to the industry of beavers; this theory is supported by several finds of beavers' bones in the rich peat deposits which were formed, peat digging being an industry of the town until about 1870.

The First Inhabitants

We now come to the first inhabitants of Newbury. In Mesolithic times a riverside people who lived mainly by fishing spread up the Kennet Valley to Newbury and beyond, and the earliest trace of human habitation of which we can be certain is due to these people. In 1920 a Mesolithic "Flint Factory" between the sewage outfall works and the river east of the town was investigated by Mr. Peake and Mr. O. G. S. Crawford. Further excavations, carried out under the auspices of the Reading Museum and Art Gallery, the Borough Museum, Newbury, and the Newbury and District Field Club, during the years 1958 to 1961, indicate an approximate date of 7,000 B.C. for the earliest Mesolithic occupation of this area between Newbury and Thatcham. Again, when improvements were being carried out in Victoria Park in 1933-34, a considerable number of Mesolithic implements were found and further evidence of Mesolithic occupation has been discovered at Speen Moor to the west of the Lambourn Railway bridge. In 1876 and during the town drainage operations of 1894-5, Mr. Walter Money and Mr. Percy Richards made several discoveries ascribed to the Mesolithic or Neolithic periods, they refer to "Pile structures found in Bartholomew Street, Market Place, and Cheap Street not far from the Kennet". These various discoveries show that the valley at Newbury was thinly inhabited by a poor and primitive fishing people some six or seven thousand years ago.

The Neolithic Age *(Before c. 1,850 B.C.)*

The next period, the Neolithic or New Stone Age, was one of great importance for it brought the "Dawn of Agriculture". Newcomers, known as Neolithic A people, arrived in this country from the continent. They were a pastoral people and kept cattle on the open chalk lands. The Neolithic A people were almost certainly the first to use the great trackway known as the Old Way which runs from the Channel near Dover to Salisbury Plain. The course of this green road from Farnham to Salisbury Plain has been described by Mr. Coghlan and Mr. Maguire. (Trans. Newbury Field Club, vii, No. 3 and viii, No. 1). The Old Way is not far to the south of Newbury where it runs along the ridge on the south side of Kingsclere and then by the Seven Barrows and Three Legged Cross to Walbury Hill. Shortly after this, other Neolithic people arrived who grew grain and who did not keep exclusively to the chalk lands. The Newbury district was becoming more populated for Neolithic tools and pottery, while not common, have been frequently found. To the north of Newbury is the ancient track known as the Berkshire Ridgeway. It runs from Salisbury Plain, past Avebury, along the northern scarp of the Berkshire Downs, to reach the Thames at Streatley. The Ridgeway as a beaten track is later than the Old Way; its full use may have delayed until Bronze Age times though it is suggestive that, at its Streatley end, it leads to a great through track to the chalk of Lincolnshire and beyond.

The Bronze and Iron Ages *(Bronze before c. 500 B.C.)* *(Iron after c. 500 B.C.)*

In the Bronze and Iron Ages, population again intensified. A large number of Bronze Age relics has been described and illustrated by Mrs. Roskill (Trans. Newbury Field Club viii, No. 1), among those found at Newbury are a flat axe, four palstaves, and a number of spears. Two of these spear heads were found at Speen Moor and one in the Lambourn railway cutting, near the supposed early river crossing; another was found in Victoria Park. Tumuli on Wash Common have the appearance of Round Barrows of this period. Through the kindness of D. B. Waterhouse, Esq., the very important hoard of Bronze Age implements, found during the erection of Yattendon Court, Yattendon, in 1876, and unique in Berkshire, is now displayed in the Newbury Museum. In the Bronze Age, communications improved and a number of roads between the two great ridge trackways (The Old Way and The Berkshire Ridgeway), are no doubt of Bronze Age date. On the north side of Newbury, Old Street ran from the Ridgeway by Lands End and Oareborough to Faircross and from there Long Lane led to Speenhamland and Newbury by Shaw Crescent. A western branch of Old Street ran from the east side of Peasemore through Winterbourne. As it then passes down the valley it may have been a track for summer use; but if it continued south through Speen it reaches the spot where Mr. Peake considered the first river crossing to have been, between Speen Moor and the Lambourn Railway bridge. In his opinion the Bronze Age track ran south from here by Enborne Gate Farm on the line of the old Borough Boundary, and then on the course of the footpath along the present boundary. Crossing Essex Street, it continued by Battle Road and the Wash Common burial mounds, on the old course of the boundary, and crossed the River Enborne to the west of the Woodpecker, joining the "Honey Way" which led to the Three Legged Cross. There is still a grassy track which can be followed for nearly a mile to the south of the burial mounds, but it disappears in a copse before reaching the Enborne. Mr. Peake also considered the two other ancient tracks from the south on the course of the present Winchester and Basingstoke Roads originally converged towards the west end of Pound Street and continued west to the early Kennet crossing near Speen Moor; and that another Bronze Age track ran north-west along the ridge between the Kennet and Lambourn valleys. Though the main Bath Road is comparatively modern, the section from Speen Lane by Oxford Street and London Road to Shaw Crescent through Speenhamland must date from this period. Among other roads which probably date from the Bronze Age is the road from Faircross by Yattendon and Ashampstead Common to Pangbourne, and also several branches of the Ridgeway. The river crossing was probably moved to its present position in the centre of Newbury at some time in the Iron Age, when the technique of river crossing was much developed. The roads from the south changed more onto their present courses, but the Andover Road ran on the west side of the Hospital to the City and then by Argyle Road and Bartholomew Street to Northbrook Street. The Winchester Road ran by the Old Newtown Road on the west side of the Cemetery and then by Derby Road to join the Andover Road at the City. The Basingstoke Road ran down Pyle Hill and by Cheap Street to the river crossing at the south end of Northbrook Street;

Iron Age Relics and Hill Forts. *(After c. 500 B.C.)*

Space does not permit a detailed description of the Iron Age relics found in, and around, Newbury. Specimens from this and other periods may be inspected in the Newbury Museum. A number of Iron Age Hill-forts may be seen on the hill-tops to north and south, the nearest being Grimsbury, Borough Hill, Walbury, Beacon Hill, and Ladle Hill. Excavation has shown that there was a large earthwork still closer, at Ramsbury Corner near Cold Ash.

Roman Occupation. *(A.D. 43 to 410)*

During the Roman occupation of Britain there was an important station on the great Roman Road from Silchester to Cirencester at Spinae which is presumed to have been near the village of Speen. Traces have been found of an important Roman settlement at Newtown by Thatcham; and there can be no doubt that a considerable settlement existed at Newbury. Though no actual buildings have yet been discovered, numerous other Roman relics have been found in and around the town and notably in the vicinity of the Market Place; while there was a Roman cemetery near the goods shed to the north of the railway. Evidence of Roman roads have been found in Newtown Road, Bartholomew Street, Northbrook Street, Shaw Road and near The Chestnuts between the Oxford and the Bath Roads.

The Early Manor.

Nothing is known of Newbury during The Dark Ages; but it appears to have continued as an important settlement and in the reign of Edward the Confessor it had become a flourishing town of traders and wayfarers at the easy ford where so many roads converged. The manor was then called Ulvritone and it was held of the king by Ulward the White. At the time of the Domesday Survey, there were two mills and the manor was held by Ernulf of Hesding. Ernulf would appear to have been an important officer in William the Conqueror's invading Norman army as he was granted no less than 47 other manors in England by the king. He was later unjustly accused before the king, and though proving himself innocent by combat, he gave up his manors to join a pilgrimage to the Holy Land in 1096 but he died when he arrived at Antioch.

The Name.

Much of the town then lay in the parish of Speen, and the name Newbury was doubtless given to distinguish it from the old Village. The name Newbury first appears in a document relating to the priory of Auffay in the diocese of Rouen. In 1079, Gilbert de Heugleville deposited before the altar there a gift of certain English property which included the church of Speen and revenues from Newbury. This priory of Auffay was originally a house of regular canons, but Gilbert refounded it in 1067 as a dependency of the great Benedictine abbey at St. Evroult. A few years later the church of St. Nicolas at Newbury was granted to the abbey of Preaux by Ernulf de Hesding. This church was claimed as a chapelry by Thatcham, the neighbouring borough town; and the parish and borough of Newbury were carved out of the parishes of Thatcham and Speen at a later date.

The Early Borough.

It would appear that Newbury already had an independent standing before it received its own boundaries, and that it probably had burghal rights from very early times. But the first documentary evidence of the borough to be found is in the Pipe Roll in 1189, where Burgesses of Newbury are mentioned. A number of other references to the borough appear in records throughout the 13th century.

The Middle Ages

The Castle.

There is no record of when the Castle at the Wharf was built; but this castle was captured by Stephen in 1152-53, after a siege of over two months. The castle was defended for Matilda by John Marshall who had to hand over his son William as a hostage. According to the contemporary poem, which is partly quoted in Money's History of Newbury, Stephen threatened William with many forms of death; but the boy survived to become famous in history as the Earl of Pembroke and the Great Protector. Ruins of the Castle were standing in 1672, and at least a portion of the castle was occupied for habitation in 1692, as is shown by a rent for encroachment in the hands of the Borough Archivist. Stone buildings at the Wharf were said to be built from the materials of the demolished castle, as nearly all other domestic buildings in the town are of brick. One stone building still remains, by the Car Park.

King John.

King John was intimately connected with Newbury, which he visited in 1200, accompanied by his natural son, Geoffrey. When King Philip of France confiscated his possessions in Normandy, John retaliated by seizing the possessions of Normans in England and in 1204 he took Newbury into his own hands, bestowing it upon Robert FitzRoger. According to a legend, John was hidden in the cottage of an old Newbury spinning woman when he fled from the insurgent barons.

Manor and Borough 12th - 14th Century.

The manor had passed to the Chaworths, and was held by Payne de Montdublel of that family in 1166. After many vicissitudes it was ceded by the brother and heir of the Count of Perche, who fell at the battle of Lincoln in 1217, to the Salisbury and Marshall families. Soon after this the borough and manor passed to William

Marshall, Earl of Pembroke, the son of the Great Protector, and after him to his brothers, each dying without issue. Eleanor, William's widow and the sister of the king, married Simon de Montfort in 1238 and he was in possession until his death at the battle of Evesham in 1265, when the borough passed to Gilbert, Earl of Gloucester. After 1274, it returned, sub-divided, to the female line of the Marshall family. In the following year the borough sent two members to Parliament and Newbury had become one of the great English centres of craftsmen. After 1316, the house of Mortimer became the chief holders of land and manorial rights in Newbury; but in that year the town is not mentioned among the Berkshire boroughs which was possibly due to a decline in trade. In the early 15th century, Newbury was held by Edmund Mortimer, Earl of March. He died without issue in 1425, and Newbury passed to his sister's son, Richard, Duke of York.

The Wars of the Roses.

This involved Newbury in the Wars of the Roses, and the town was taken by the Earl of Wiltshire in 1460, when many of the inhabitants were executed as traitors for supporting the White Rose and the other townsmen were deprived of all their possessions. Richard fell at Wakefield in the same year, and his son became King Edward IV in the following year when Newbury was regarded as a royal appanage. The town was one of the meeting places for Buckingham's rising in 1483.

Borough Charter.

Henry VIII granted Newbury to Anne Boleyn and Jane Seymour in turn, and Edward VI granted it to his sister Elizabeth, later Queen, who made her first visit in 1568 and who granted the earliest existing Charter to the Borough in 1596. That this was not the first Charter is proved by a reference to an earlier Charter in the preamble. James I granted Newbury to his queen, Anne of Denmark, and they both visited the town in 1603, the year before the plague which carried off a great number of the inhabitants. At last, in 1627, Charles I granted the lordship and manorial rights to the mayor and corporation in return for a quit-rent.

Religious Houses, Greenham.

There are no visible remains of Greenham Preceptory of Knights Hospitallers which stood on the north side of the new Police Station, and the medieval stone boundary wall, to the east of the car park, had to be demolished when the new road was made in 1963. Established in the reign of Henry II, the inmates in 1338 were the Preceptor, a brother knight, a chaplain, a squire, a bailiff, with several under officers and servants. Another house of this order at Shalford, near Brimpton, was run in conjunction with Greenham. The order was suppressed by Henry VIII in 1540, but Greenham was revived for a short time in the reign of Mary, to be finally suppressed when Elizabeth ascended the throne.

Sandleford.

The Priory of St. John the Baptist at Sandleford, was founded between 1193 and 1200 by Geoffrey, Count of Perche and lord of Newbury, for Augustinian Canons. It was one of the smaller priories with never more than six canons and only three in 1274. A project for increasing the endowments and turning the house into a great Benedictine convent of the order of Fontevrault for 40 nuns and 10 chaplains never materialised. Edward II stayed here in 1320, and a royal pensioner was lodged on the priory. Prior Simon Dam was deposed in 1440 being accused of allowing the house to become ruinous and of other faults. The priory never recovered and being left vacant by the death of the last canon in 1478, the estates and buildings were granted to St. George's Chapel, Windsor. The large mansion, now St. Gabriel's School, incorporates some of the old monastic walls, notably of the choir of the priory church, with its interesting timber roof, but the windows and buttresses are later replacements.

Hospital of St. Bartholomew.

It is believed that King John founded the Hospital of St. Bartholomew in Newbury, but the charter is lost; however, he granted the fair of two days in 1215 which was held annually until the last war. The hospital was for a priest warden, who is sometimes called prior, with brethren and sisters living under religious vows and caring for the aged and sick. It was not suppressed at the Reformation, and became almshouses, the present interesting range dating from 1618, while the central cupola is dated 1698. The building is of mellow red brick with a moulded cornice, and wings extend to Argyle Road on each side of the main block. In the centre is an ornamental archway above which are the Royal Arms of the 18th century.

Litten Chapel.

To the north is the 15th century chapel of the Hospital, called the Litten Chapel. It is attached to the old Grammar School, and the east end of the chapel was cut off when the Newtown Road was widened in 1825. In the north wall were formerly two square-headed windows, each of two lights, of the decorated period; but one of these has been converted into a doorway. There is a window of a later date in the south wall with a modern doorway. The gabled roof has carved and moulded queen-posts of the Tudor period with one section in the decorated style, with its tie-beams removed, and the moulded purlins have curved wind braces.

St. Mary's.

Another hospital, dedicated to St. Mary Magdalen for leprous women, is recorded in 1232. It is possible that the name was changed to The House of Blessed Mary, a hospital of sisters which appears in a deed of 1375. No further records have been found and the house may have become St. Mary's Almshouses for six poor women which was in existence in 1604, and was then considered ancient.

Donnington Friary.

A Chapel of Jesus was rebuilt at Donnington by Sir Richard Abberbury after 1365, and in 1376 he granted the endowments to the Priory of the Crouched Friars in London, on condition that two friars should live there and serve the chapel. A Priory of the Crouched Friars was established, and a conventual chapel was built on the north side of the Jesus Chapel which was taken from the friars in 1448 as they had not fulfilled the conditions. The Priory was suppressed in 1538, being surrendered by two friars who claimed to be the Trinitarian Order, but this was probably a ruse through which they hoped to gain pensions. The Jesus Chapel was suppressed as a chantry in 1546. A large house called The Priory occupies the site.

Donnington Hospital.

Donnington Hospital was founded in 1393 by Sir Richard Abberbury, and stands between the bridges over the Lambourn River on the west side of the Oxford Road. It was built for 13 poor men, one of whom was to act as master with the title of God's Minister; and the inmates attended services in the chapel of the friars. One of the almsmen, Thomas Barrie, was accused in 1538 of spreading a rumour that Henry VIII was dead, and he was made to stand all day in Newbury Market Place with his ears nailed to pillory and at the end of the day both his ears were cut off. At the reformation the hospital was not suppressed, but the revenues were confiscated by the crown. Queen Elizabeth restored the revenues in 1570, and with the Earl of Nottingham she refounded the almshouses as "The Hospital of Queen Elizabeth", in 1602. The picturesque buildings date from that year and form a square with an open court in the middle. The buildings are of red brick with massive chimney stacks, and a covered walk runs round the court in the form of a cloister. A good deal of restoration has been necessary and the porch is a later addition. Above the doorway are the gilded arms of Queen Elizabeth and inside the porch are the old weathered stone arms which were originally on the font.

Donnington Castle.

Sir Richard Abberbury also rebuilt Donnington Castle after he had received the necessary royal licence in 1386. Edward VI stayed here in 1552, and Queen Elizabeth granted the castle to the Earl of Nottingham, Baron Howard of Effingham, in 1600, as a reward for services in the Spanish Armada. The story of the gallant defence of the castle by Colonel Sir John Boys during the Civil War will be found later under the battles of Newbury. The great Gate House remains to almost its full height and is one of the finest examples of fourteenth century military architecture in England. It is built of flint with stone dressings and consists of three main storeys with tall circular flanking towers on each side of the main gateway. The archway of the gate is four-centred with a label. The string-courses are ornamental with grotesque heads. The walls have been pitted in a number of places by the cannonballs fired during the sieges and brick patching has been necessary in places. A cottage which was built on to the back in the 19th century has been demolished. The entrance way on the ground floor has lovely and intricate stone vaulting springing from attached shafts. A newel stair in the southern flanking tower leads to the upper floors. The first floor has a large square-headed window retaining some of its tracery. A number of important buildings were formerly attached to the west side of the gate-house which probably included the great hall on the first floor, and in the wall are several doorways, fireplaces and windows. The

Donnington Castle.

foundations of the curtain walls can be traced to the west, and the castle was originally some 150 feet long and 93 feet wide. Works of preservation were recently carried out by the Department of the Environment.

Winchester College Hostelry.

A hostelry was established in Newbury in the mid-15th century by Winchester College for students and travellers between Winchester and New College, Oxford. It stood in Northcroft Lane facing Pembroke Road and was a long medieval building of two storeys. Parts of this building were considered to date from the 13th century and to have been relics of a still earlier hostelry possibly established by King John but first recorded in 1223 as belonging to Henry III. The whole building was pulled down in 1934 (Trans. Newbury Field Club, vii 3). Winchester College had other property in Newbury, notably a house on the west side of Northbrook Street and two houses and gardens in West Street (the old name of Bartholomew Street) backing on Rockingham, a lane that formerly ran behind Bartholomew Street from West Mills.

Grammar School.

In 1466, Henry Wormestall founded a chantry in the parish church, the priest "techyng a gramer scole ther"; and this appears to be the origin of Newbury Grammar School. The chantry was suppressed in the reign of Edward VI, but the school continued under its master in the Litten Chapel until 1814. A larger school, The Old Grammar School, was built attached to this chapel in 1884, and in 1885 it was transferred to the present spacious site to the south of the Enborne Road. See also page 60.

The Late Middle Ages and the Cloth Trade

The prosperity and trade of Newbury grew in the 15th century when the town became world-famous for its weaving. The principal business centres were the Market Place which had stallages and shambles, the old wooden bridge over the Kennet, which had shops upon it, and Northbrook Street.

Jack of Newbury.

Towards the end of this century, the cloth trade produced Newbury's greatest hero, John Smallwood, who changed his name to John Winchcombe and who became known as "Jack of Newbury". Jack is believed to have been born at Winchcombe in Gloucestershire and when he had reached the age of fifteen his parents sent him to the great abbey there with the view that he should become a monk. But before he had taken any vows he felt that he was not at all suited to a celibate monastic life and so he ran away. Coming to Newbury, he was apprenticed to a rich cloth-maker, and when his master died he married Alice, the wealthy young widow. It appears that the two had been indulging in a mild flirtation during the master's lifetime, and after Alice became a widow, she chose Jack, though there were many more prosperous suitors; and the wedding took place in the Litten Chapel. It was not a very happy match as Alice was both gay and frivolous, and there is a story that one night when she came home very late, Jack refused to let her in. At last he relented to her entreaties; but when he had let her in she pretended that she had dropped her ring outside. When Jack kindly went out to look for it she slammed the door and locked it, keeping him outside in his night-shirt for the remainder of the night. Before long Alice died, leaving all her wealth and the flourishing business to Jack. But he soon married again, this time Joan, the daughter of a poor man from Aylesbury; but a most sumptuous wedding took place. Jack extended the cloth-making business to such a degree that he may be said to have erected the first true factory in England, with 200 looms

Jack of Newbury - from the brass in St. Nicolas Church.

and employing nearly 1,000 men, women and children. The factory stretched from his house in Northbrook Street to the Marsh, now Victoria Park. Jack was ordered to provide four pikemen and two horsemen for the King's army during the war with Scotland. But he gathered and equipped a force of 50 pikemen and 50 horsemen, leading them in person. A contemporary poem tells how the lads of Newbury distinguished themselves at the battle of Flodden in 1513, and there appears to be no doubt that this was the case, though certain writers have maintained that the Newbury force was not in time for the battle. Jack entertained Henry VIII and his first queen, Catherine of Aragon (1516 - 18) when the king wished to dub him knight, but Jack begged to be excused the honour as he preferred to remain a plain man among his work people. Jack died soon afterwards in 1519, and was succeeded by his son, John Winchcombe, to whom Henry VIII granted the Bucklebury estates of Reading Abbey in 1540. A portrait of the son of Jack can be seen in the Municipal Buildings and a copy at the Museum.

Jack of Newbury's House.

Jack of Newbury's House in Northbrook Street has been partly re-modelled for shops but the lovely north end remains on Marsh Lane. This gable end is built of brick with timber framing. The first floor overhangs the street and has delicate carved bracket and moulded woodwork ornamented with carving. The space between the timbers is filled with bricks in herringbone pattern and there is a delightful oriel window with moulded framing. The gable again overhangs above this and has barge-boards. Inside there is not much to see, but several details of the 16th century remain, and the roof and a chimney stack are part of the original building.

The Parish Church of St. Nicolas.

The Church of St. Nicolas is first mentioned in the Hyde Chronicles of the late 11th century, and it was probably built by Ernulf de Hesding who granted the Church and the Priest's House to Preaux Abbey. This Norman Church apparently remained in use until the end of the 15th century, when it was pulled down and rebuilt on a larger scale. There are no remains of the Norman Church, but some foundations were unearthed on the north of the present nave some years ago and their date caused some dispute. The fine Perpendicular Church as it is seen today was built largely through the munificence of Jack of Newbury and his son, between about 1500

Jack of Newbury's house, Northbrook Street.

and 1532, the latter date appearing on the tower which was the last part of the building to be completed. It is one of the best and most complete churches of the period, and very few modern alterations have been made. These include an extension to the north chapel to form a vestry, the arches opening into the side chapels from the chancel, the chancel roof, the chancel arch, the embattled parapets, and the pinnacles to the turrets of the tower, all these alterations being made between 1850 and 1870. The Church is 148 feet long and consists of a chancel with north and south chapels, an aisled nave of five bays with north and south porches, and a western tower. The nave arcades have clustered pillars and richly moulded arches with a hoof-mould over. All the pillars are of similar design except the second from the east on the north side which appears to be older than the rest. All the windows are filled with good Perpendicular tracery. The nave and aisle roofs have had to be restored in places and the bosses are carved with various designs, a number having J.S. for John Smallwood. In the nave roof there are moulded tie beams with curved braces whose spandrels are filled with tracery and which spring from the walls resting on modern corbels. The chapels on each side of the chancel are lit by windows of three lights, but the east

St. Nicolas Church in the late eighteenth century.

window of the north chapel was moved to the east end of the vestry when this was built. The east window of the chancel is of six lights. The reredos and sedilia are modern. The windows of the church contain some good modern glass. The tower is of three stages, with octagonal turrets at the corners and there is a peal of ten bells. Below the tower is the brass of Jack of Newbury, 1519, and he is depicted wearing a furred cloak with a belt and pouch, his wife is beside him, and below are his two sons and daughter. There are four later brasses of 1595 and 1641; and against the outside of the south wall of the chancel is a large tomb of 1587. Under one arch is depicted Griffith Curteys who is kneeling and wearing half-armour with a ruff, under the other arch are three wives, and below are six boys and five girls. Griffith Curteys helped to endow the Church Almshouses in 1583. There are a number of other old memorials on the church walls and in the graveyard. The fine early Jacobean pulpit was given to the church by Margaret Cross in 1607 and the font is modern. There were three chantries attached to the church, and these were suppressed in 1546 with a chapel at the north end of Northbrook Street and a Guild of St. George.

The Reformation

Apart from the suppression of the religious houses and chantries, Newbury did not suffer great persecution at the Reformation. The poor old inmate of Donnington Hospital who had his ears cut off after standing with them nailed to the pillory in Newbury Market Place has already been mentioned. Miles Coverdale, one of Thomas Cromwell's zealous informers, wrote from Newbury that the priests were not energetic enough in carrying out the religious reforms, and about certain popish books he had found; and it is interesting to note that his second letter was carried by "young Mr. Winchcombe".

The Newbury Martyrs.

During the religious persecution in the reign of Queen Mary, Jocelyn Palmer, the young master of Reading Grammar School and former fellow of Magdalen College, Oxford, was tried for heresy and condemned in the parish Church, with Thomas Askew and John Gwyn, a weaver. They were burnt at the stake at the Sandpits by the Enborne Road, in 1556.

Shaw House and The Dolmans.

A Guild of Weavers is believed to have existed in Newbury at an

The Old Cloth Hall c1790. Now the Museum.

early date, and it was revived after the Elizabeth Charter as a Company. After Jack of Newbury's death, his manager, William Dolman, appears to have set up for himself. His son, Thomas Dolman, acquired such wealth through clothmaking that he bought the manor of Shaw in 1554. Retiring from business, he began to build Shaw House on a huge scale. But he died in 1575 before it was completed, and the house was finished by his son, John, in 1581. Dolman's retirement helped the decline in the cloth trade which began in 1564 and there was much unemployment in Newbury. So when the great house was built, the townsmen expressed their feelings with the rhyme :

"Lord have mercy upon us sinners!
Thomas Dolman has built a new house and
has turned away all his spinners!"

Dolman retorted with a Latin inscription on the portico of his house meaning :

"The toothless one envies the eaters teeth,
And the mole scorns the she-goats eyes".

and on the frieze of the porch, a Greek inscription, meaning:

"Let no jealous person enter here".

The house is one of the finest Elizabethan mansions in the country, and is built of red brick with quoins, string-courses, and mullioned windows. It is of two main storeys with a third gabled storey under the tiled roofs. The rooms contain some fine oak panelling and the great staircase has a moulded handrail supported by twisted ballusters. There are a number of stone fireplaces throughout the house which now forms part of Shaw House Comprehensive School.

Kendrick's Charity.

In 1624, John Kendrick left the then huge sum of £4,000 which was to be partly invested in a house and garden and partly to form a fund to provide work for the poor. The Corporation of Newbury bought a site called The Castle, with an acre of meadow adjoining, called Hospital Mead, probably taking its name from the site of the Preceptory of Knights Hospitallers nearby.

Work was begun on the house in 1627, and it is recorded that a part of the old castle was still standing at that time. Some of the timber was used for doing repairs to the parish church and some of the stone may have been used for building the place of work.

This house of work – in modern terms, a cloth factory (later called the Cloth Hall), enabled 14 boys and girls to be apprenticed and 60 poor people to be employed in the cloth trade, while it gave spinning work to 50 poor households. In 1630, a hungry mob stopped and looted the corn carts going from Newbury to Reading, and, though the ring-leaders were mostly from Speen and Greenham, a number of old Newbury women were punished. Among steps taken to deal with the distress was the closing of 27 alehouses.

Guildhall.

Nearby, in the middle of the Market Place, stood the old Guildhall which was erected in 1611. To the south was the market cross and in 1684 a prison was built on the east side. The upper floor of the Guildhall was reached by stairs from the pavement. The Quarter Sessions were held in the Council Chamber on the first floor and beneath, on the ground floor, were the whipping post, the stocks, and the pillory. Stallholders sold their wares under the shelter of the building which stood on pillars. It was demolished in 1828.

The Civil War

Newbury was a place of great strategical importance to both sides during the Civil War, owing to its position between London and the south, and two of the principal battles were fought close to the town. When the war started in August, 1642, the rural areas around Newbury were on the side of Charles I, but there were many Presbyterians in the town and a large number of the townsmen favoured Parliament. His first victory at Edgehill brought Charles to the gates of London but he was held at Turnham Green and retired on Oxford. His three armies were widely scattered and Essex besieged and captured Reading for Parliament in April, 1643; but he was too weak to advance on Oxford. The Royalist armies then had a number of successes in the west, and Bristol was captured. Charles started to besiege Gloucester hoping to secure another western base, and Essex moved west with a strong relieving force from London. Hearing of this army's approach, Charles raised the siege and, having his main base at Oxford, he realised that he might be able to cut off the army of Essex from London. A surprise attack on a Royalist force at Cirencester made Essex aware of this danger, and he began to withdraw his army at all speed through Wiltshire, meaning to return to London by Newbury and Reading. While the Royalist army marched by Faringdon and Wantage, Rupert harrassed the Parliamentary army with his cavalry and a minor battle was fought near Aldbourne.

First Battle of Newbury.

Essex reached Enborne on 19th September, 1643, to find that the Royalist army had already reached Newbury and was drawn up on The Wash across his line of retreat. Realising that he was now in a perilous position as supplies were running short, while his men were hungry, tired and wet after a long march through the rain, he drew his army up for the night on the line of Crockham Heath; and he decided that the only way to save the situation was to attack and break through the Royalists on the following day. His army was some eight thousand strong, while the Royalists numbered about ten thousand. Essex deployed his army at dawn on the 20th September. He placed his right wing under Skippon in front of Biggs Hill, facing Rupert and his cavalry; his main body and artillery on the plateau to the west of Wheatlands Farm and Cope Hall, facing Charles's main body and guns which were drawn up on The Wash; and his left wing with a grand reserve, under Robartes, covered Enborne Village and Hamstead Park, facing the King's Life Guards under Byron. The Rivers Kennet and Enborne formed a protection to the flanks of both armies. Charles's position was well chosen; but Essex at once observed that the round hill above Cope Hall had not been occupied and might prove the key to victory as it commanded the lower slopes between The Wash and Newbury. He therefore pushed a strong force forward on this hill while his left wing attacked. Skippon advanced his right wing in support, and the Cavaliers charged down upon the Roundheads in spite of Charles's orders for defensive action. Skippon's force was driven right back but retreated in good order and some of the Cavaliers found themselves isolated and had to fight their way out while Charles attacked on the right to relieve the pressure. Essex had meanwhile been attacking in the centre and trying to press forward from the round hill. But the Royalist attacks drove his men back from the hill and confused fighting went on for a long time in the narrow lanes around Skinners Green. Essex then rallied his men for a supreme attack. By a gallant charge they recaptured the round hill, and pressing on, gained a footing on The Wash. The king rushed all his available reserves to the spot to prevent a breakthrough, and the fiercest fighting now took place on the ridge in the vicinity of the Burial Mounds and to the north of Essex Street. Rupert was now trying to retrieve the day by further attacks on Skippon's force, but with great loss of life; and to the north both sides were impeded by the ditches, banks and hedges near the Kennet. Fighting went on well into the night until at last both sides had to draw back to rest. The Roundheads were cheerless, tired, hungry, and without water, and their chances in the struggle which they were expecting to begin again at dawn seemed critical to Charles. His gunpowder was nearly exhausted, his losses in officers and men had been terrible, and exaggerated reports came in about the size of the army of Essex. So, when Essex began to prepare for further attacks at dawn on the following day, he found the Royalist army had disappeared during the night and the way to London was open. The Roundheads marched by Greenham Common and Brimpton, and near Aldermaston a fruitless attack was made upon their rearguard by Rupert's cavalry.

Lord Falkland.

Altogether some six thousand men fell in this battle, and among them were the Earls of Carnarvon and of Sunderland and Viscount Falkland. Lord Falkland was then thirty-three years old and he was so brilliant and lovable that he was admired by both Cavaliers and Roundheads. He had joined Charles though he hated the idea of war. He kept murmuring to himself "Peace! Peace" and at the siege of Gloucester had exposed himself to unnecessary risks. On the morning of the Battle of Newbury his friends had tried to persuade him to stay in the rear as he looked so ill and broken-hearted, and as he had no definite command. But he still persisted in volunteering to serve with Byron where the fighting would be thickest, telling his friends that he was weary of the times and foresaw much misery to his country, but that he believed he would be out of it ere night. After Essex had captured the round hill, Byron tried to lead his men through a gap in the hedge to drive the Roundheads back, but the gap was commanded by enemy fire and his horse was shot under him. While he was waiting for another horse to be brought, Falkland charged through the gap alone and he and his horse were immediately killed. After the battle his body was identified and carried to a farmhouse, now on the corner of Falkland Garth. A memorial was raised to his memory in 1878 and stands at the corner where Essex Street joins the Andover Road. Sixty cart loads of dead were carried into Newbury, the majority of the burials took place on the battlefield itself.

Falkland Garth.

Falkland Garth stands on the north side of Essex Street and the picturesque farmhouse, now the residences on the corner, appears to date from the first years of the 17th century. It is of red brick with a central chimney stack. The wing on the roadside was added in the 18th century and there is a more modern extension behind. The rooms on the ground floor have chamfered beams supporting the ceiling and the timbering of the roof is exposed on the landing and in a bedroom.

Burial Mounds.

There are three large burial mounds on the sides of the Recreation Ground to the south of Essex Street, but the fourth smaller mound has almost disappeared. They look like Prehistoric Round Barrows of the Bronze Age and they are the supposed burial place of most of the soldiers who were slain in this battle. Pending some archaeological excavation, the origin of the mounds must remain an open one. Newbury children used to decorate the mounds with flowers on the anniversary of the battle every year. Among the fir trees can be seen some of the lines occupied by the Royalist artillery. A number of burials were also made on the round hill above Cope Hall, which has recently been demolished.

Second Battle of Newbury

After his retirement on Oxford, the king had left a garrison at Donnington Castle under Col. John Boys. In the following months the campaigns had ended disastrously for the Royalists in the north at the Battle of Marston Moor, and the king turned his attention to the army of Essex which had been pushing into the west of England. Essex was cornered in Cornwall, but escaped by sea, leaving Skippon to negotiate the surrender of his forces. The king was at Salisbury on his way back when the opposing generals decided that they must act quickly to prevent him from marching on London or returning to Oxford, and a large army, nearly 20,000 strong, was assembled near Basingstoke and at Reading under the Earl of Manchester, Sir William Waller, and the Earl of Essex. When it was reported that Charles was returning to Oxford, it was decided to intercept him at Newbury. Essex remained behind at Reading as he was sick, and the army marched with Manchester in command, passing through Thatcham and Bucklebury in order to come on Newbury from the north-east and hoping to take the Cavaliers by surprise. But Charles had already joined forces with Col. Boys who was holding Donnington Castle and Shaw House. The Royalists' forces were greatly outnumbered being only about 10,000 strong, but they took up defensive positions in readiness for any attack. The main body of cavalry and artillery was placed in the fields between Speenhamland and the River Lambourn, protected from the north-west by the strong fortifications around Donnington Castle and from the north-east by fortifications in the grounds of Shaw House, while the village of Shaw was fortified by a breastwork. Strong guards were placed to the east and to the south of the town. A strong force under Prince Maurice was posted to the west at Speen and Speen Hill with a smaller force with four guns protecting the flank near Deanwood and small outposts at the Bagnor and Boxford fords. So, when Manchester approached Newbury from the north-east, he found it strongly defended instead of open as he had hoped. His great army was assembled in the area Cold Ash, Ashmore Green, and Clay Hill, from which he and his commanders surveyed the Royalists' dispositions. It was decided that an out-flanking movement was necessary so as to develop main attacks both on Speen and Shaw; and on the 26th October, a large force was sent out under Skippon, who was again in the field, Waller and Cromwell. This force marched by Hermitage and Chieveley, resting for the night at North Heath. The march was continued at dawn on the following day by Boxford, where there was a short skirmish, Wickham Heath, and Stockcross, where the Roundheads deployed for their main attack on Speen and Speen Hill. It had been arranged that Manchester should open his main attack on Shaw as soon as he heard cannon fire from the Speen direction. The battle opened soon after dawn on 27th October, 1644, by Manchester making a small reconnaissance attack with a force of 400 musketeers who attempted to cross the River Lambourn by a temporary bridge; but this attack was driven off with loss and several men were drowned: Little further fighting took place until well into the afternoon, when the outflanking force began to develop the attack from the west. The Royalists were taken by surprise, their cavalry reserve was away foraging, and they were hopelessly outnumbered. The Roundheads over-ran their breast-works and guns and swept forward with the Royalists in full flight towards Donnington and Newbury. The king had watched this rout and was trying to rally his men when Sir John Cansfield and Sir Humphrey Bennet led gallant cavalry charges which drove the Roundheads back. Heavy fighting continued until nightfall in the fields between Newbury and Donnington, but the Roundheads were unable to make further headway and finally retired into Speen. Though Manchester had heard gunfire when this action opened, he appears to have delayed his main attack until he saw the routed Cavaliers retreating into Newbury. At last he marched his men down Clay Hill, singing psalms as they went, to the attack upon Shaw and Shaw House. The Cavaliers were driven back behind the defences in the grounds of Shaw House and here an intense and fluctuating struggle continued for a long time. At last Royalist reinforcements arrived and the Roundheads fled back up Clay Hill hotly pursued by the Cavaliers, who were led by Astley, Brown, Lisle, Page and Thelwell. Manchester made another attack before darkness fell, but this was again driven back with great loss. Having watched the rout of his troops at Speen, Charles considered that he could not hope to continue to hold his position at Newbury against such odds; and he ordered his main army to retire to Oxford while he turned west to Bath with a small escort. Manchester, who had seen one attack after another repulsed at Shaw House, offered no opposition to the Royalist withdrawals until a wordy argument with Cromwell forced him reluctantly to agree to a pursuit; but by then it was too late to catch up with the king's retreating army.

Sieges of Donnington Castle.

Charles had left most of his artillery behind at Donnington Castle which was again besieged by the Roundheads. The previous siege had begun in August, over two months before the Second Battle of Newbury, the castle then being owned by John Packer and defended by Sir John Boys, whose portrait is in the Municipal Buildings. Gen. Middleton was in command of the Roundheads, and he summoned the castle to surrender; but Boys replied that he would maintain his trust. In an assault of six hours the Roundheads lost over 100 men and were driven off by a gallant sally. Another strong assault was made on 19th September by Col. Horton who succeeded in beating down three of the towers of the curtain wall. The castle was again summoned to surrender with the threat that no life would be spared unless it did so. Boys replied that he would keep the place and neither take nor give quarter. On that night he made another sally, and drove the besiegers back with great loss. After the futile pursuit of the king's army following the Second Battle, Manchester was ordered to return to Donnington with his entire army to capture the castle which was encircled on 7th November. The castle was again summoned to surrender with the threat that if it continued to hold out no stone would be left standing upon another. Boys replied that he was not bound to repair the castle walls, but with God's help he would keep the ground it stood on. Siege pieces had been brought from London, and a strong assault was made and driven off, after which the Roundheads retired into Newbury. Two days later, Charles, who had returned to Oxford with Prince Rupert and

Donnington Castle - a besieger's view.

reinforcements from Bath, relieved Donnington Castle with an army of about 10,000 men. He collected the artillery he had left behind and then marched down the hill, crossed the River Lambourn, and paraded in front of the Roundheads in Newbury with drums beating, trumpets sounding, and colours flying. The Roundhead army just looked on and made excuses for not accepting his challenge; and Charles returned to the castle where he spent the night. He marched away to the west by Lambourn and Marlborough on the following day, and Sir John Boys was again besieged. Boys continued to hold the castle until he received orders to surrender from the king who was about to give himself up to the Scottish army at Southwell, and the gallant garrison marched out with full military honours in April, 1646.

Later 17th Century.

The Civil War had brought distress and ruin to many of the Newbury people, and the quartering of Dutch prisoners on the town during the war with Holland proved an additional expense. John Kensey, a Newbury surgeon, was executed for taking part in a Royalist rising at Salisbury in 1655, and a number of officials were displaced for having supported the king's cause. Among them was Gabriel Cox, formerly mayor and then town clerk, who later accused his successor of destroying the town books.

1660-1800

Charter of Charles II

After the restoration, Charles II granted a new charter, and this strengthened the royalist element. Some of the former prosperity returned, and the Company of Clothiers and Hatters used to parade from the church to the Globe Inn after service, with the "town music" in front, then the men, and lastly the women, all in their best clothes.

Almshouses

Several almshouses were established between 1671 and 1790, by Thomas Pearce, Francis Coxedd, Philip Jemmet, Thomas Hunt, Benjamin Robinson, and John Kimber. The largest of these was Raymond's Almshouses established before 1676, by Philip Jemmet, and further endowed by his son-in-law and daughter, Sir Jonathan and Lady Raymond. Jemmet's original foundation was for 12 almspeople, and the number was later increased to 22. The almshouses were at first in the old building on the west side of Argyle Road, but they were moved to the east side of the Newtown Road in 1796 with a later extension south of the Christian Science Church.

Religion

There were already a number of Non-conformists in Newbury at the beginning of the Civil War, and the sympathies of many of the churchgoers were with the Puritans. This led to riots over the election of a churchwarden, in 1664, but threats of calling in soldiers brought a temporary truce. A Presbyterian, William Milton, was the ringleader, and when he was being questioned, his followers rose and attempted to rescue him. But the troops prevented this, and Milton was sent to London with a number of others for trial. After this event, the number of practising Non-conformists was given as only 40. The Quakers had become established in the town by 1683, and their meeting house stood back from Bartholomew Street on the west side. Now they meet on Sunday mornings at No. 1 Highfield Avenue. The Presbyterians moved their meeting house from Bartholomew Street to the Waterside Chapel in 1697, and this date was upon the wall. This old chapel was most picturesque with its mellow red-brick walls, moulded cornice, and gabled roofs. Recently, owing to disrepair, it unfortunately had to be demolished. The Independents built their first chapel in 1717, and other demoninations had early chapels which have mostly been rebuilt in more modern times.

The Newbury Skirmish

Another riot, called the Newbury Skirmish, took place in 1706. Two sergeants were sent to apprehend an idle fellow named John Pinfold for service, but as he was being led away, friends came to his help, one of the sergeants was knocked down, and he was rescued. Soldiers arrived on the scene, and he was recaptured to be again rescued by a mob which was increasing rapidly. Pinfold was again seized, and was being led away when the angry mob attacked the soldiers and a sergeant was killed. The constable and watchman had sided with the mob, but some officers came to the rescue with swords and pistols, and many of the rioters fell.

Education

Apart from the Grammar School, there were few facilities for education at the beginning of the 18th century. Francis Coxedd had left a large sum of money to be used, partly for almshouses and partly for educating children. In 1706, the Corporation used some of this money to endow a charity school for 20 poor boys under the name Kendricks School. Richard Cowslade added to this foundation in 1715, and other charity schools followed. Through the benefactions of John and Frances West, Newbury has been privileged since 1728 to send children to be educated at Christ's Hospital, one of the best public schools in the country. Special grants are also available from the same bequest. The scheme has been varied both in regard to administration and the number of places. At present several boys are receiving education at Horsham and several girls at Hertford.

Roads and Coaching.

Nearly all the roads in England were in a very bad state in the 17th

The Pelican Inn, c1800.

century, and the main highways were narrow. The old road from Bath to London ran by the narrow Back Way at Speen and after passing through Speenhamland, it followed Shaw Road to the old ford over Lambourn at Shaw and turned east up Clay Hill. It continued by the narrow "Turnpike Road" to Thatcham Gate, near the French Gardens, where it joins the present road. The Basingstoke Road was by way of Stroud Green and Pyle Hill; and the Winchester Road ran by Argyle Road, Derby Road, and the Old Newtown Road on the west side of the cemetery. The Andover Road ran by Argyle Road and Hampton Road, and then on the west side of the Hospital to join the present Andover Road at the south corner of the Recreation Ground. Travelling conditions began to improve in the late 17th century. Stage coaches ran from Windsor to London in 1673, and a few years later from Bath to London. These, of course, did not run through Newbury itself, but through Speenhamland which was not then in the borough. Many large inns sprang up here and Speenhamland became one of the most famous coaching centres in England. The older stage coaches had no springs, and were very bumpy and uncomfortable. But in 1752, The Flying Coach with its body slung on leather springs, began running from The White Hart in Newbury. It did the journey to London in 12 hours, and the fare was 10/-. The later coaches had iron springs, and after 1832, steam coaches were occasionally to be seen, but the horse-drawn coach was not supplanted until the advent of the railways.

Canals

The River Kennet was made navigable for barges from Newbury to Reading between 1714 and 1721, and in 1723 the waterway was let to the Kennet Navigation Company on a 99 year lease. The course of the river was improved in 1730, and the Wharf at Newbury became the busy depot of a very extensive barge service to London. The old wet dock is now filled in and a car park occupies some of its site, where 10 of the largest barges could formerly load and unload at a time. This waterway brought a considerable increase in trade to the town as new industries such as barge building sprang up.

Kennet and Avon Canal

The extension of this waterway to the west by the Kennet and Avon Canal was first projected in 1794. It had reached Great Bedwyn by 1801, and was completed in 1810 at a cost of £1,072,000. Barges could now go from London to Bristol, and Newbury became an important inland port. The work was planned and supervised by the eminent engineer, John Rennie, who received £350 for his services! This canal was pronounced to be one of the best inland waterways in the kingdom and, though it has been disused for many years, it could come into commercial use again. Many people consider that the transit costs for heavy goods and grain would be far cheaper by canal, and the roads would be relieved of some heavy traffic. Members of the Kennet and Avon Canal Trust Ltd. have now worked hard for several years to clear the channel and restore the locks, with the ultimate aim of having once again a navigable waterway between Bristol and London. Greenham Lock is the only "Turfed sided" lock in any borough in the country. Such locks were, and are, unique to the River Kennet Navigation and the Wey Navigation, which are pre-canal era. Newbury lock is fitted with lever operated ground paddles at its upstream end. This is the only lock (except for one near Reading, rebuilt in later times) of all the hundreds of locks in the midlands and south, fitted with this type paddle. The only other examples are said to be in Lancashire. There is a board at Newbury Lock with traditional canal painting, giving some waterway history and mentioning these paddles. On the corner of the towing path wall under W.H. Smith's shop are very good examples of grooves worn by hauling lines used by very many years of horse-drawn boat traffic.

Sandleford and Blue Stockings

In 1742, Edward Montagu, who lived at Sandleford Priory, married Elizabeth Robinson who was celebrated as being the central figure of literary society. Among their frequent visitors were Dr. Johnson, Goldsmith, and Burke. Dr. Stillingfleet used to come to her literary parties and always wore blue stockings. If he was late they used to say that they must wait for the blue stockings; and in this way the name "Blue Stockings" was acquired. Mrs. Montagu rebuilt the house after her husband's death in 1775, turning the old ruined chapel into a dining room, and the present house dates mainly from that time and is now a school. It was designed by Wyatt in the gothic style and contains some Adam decorations.

Bread Riots

A large number of poor people assembled in the Market Place on a market day in August, 1766, to demonstrate against the high price of bread. They upset sacks of corn, butchers' and other traders' stalls, so that everything was scattered in the streets. They wrecked the houses of two unpopular tradesmen, and the butchers' and provisions shops were raided. To pacify the mob the bakers reduced the price of bread by 2d. with promises of a further reduction; but the crowd then marched to Shaw Mill, where they did great damage and threw the flour into the river. Other mills were then raided, and one man was killed and several people were injured. The arrival of troops prevented further disorder, and several arrests were made, two of the ringleaders being transported. The Corporation of Newbury made good the damage which had been done.

The Kennet Bridge

For centuries there had been a wooden bridge over the Kennet at the south end of Northbrook Street, and it is recorded that this bridge needed repair in the 14th century. The old bridge had shops upon it. In 1623 the wooden bridge collapsed and was rebuilt but the new bridge was swept away in the flood of 1726, when another

Kennet Bridge, c1906.

wooden bridge was constructed. The present bridge was begun in 1769 and finished three years later. It was designed by James Clarke and cost over £700. The bridge is of a single span, with stone dressings and ballustrades. On each of the four corners are decorated stone arches supported by pilaster. Three of these arches have been incorporated in the adjoining shops, while the fourth forms a doorway to the building on the south-west side of the bridge. The strength of the bridge was proved during the last war when vehicles and tanks of the heaviest types were perpetually crossing. The views of the bridge from the riverside are delightful, and have been drawn by many famous artists. A path leads down on the east side by the Old Rectory, and an opening on the west side between W. H. Smith's shop and the Golden Egg Restaurant leads to a passage which passes under a building and then to the towing path providing a walk between London and Bristol.

Speenhamland Act

The Berkshire magistrates met at the George and Pelican, Speenhamland on 6th May, 1795, to settle the scale of relief that should be given to the poor. This became known as The Speenhamland Act, as the scale they fixed became general all over England.

The Nineteenth Century

Weaving

The cloth trade continued to decline after the mid-18th century in spite of the introduction of water power and machinery; but Newbury could not compete with the greater factories in the north.

The Newbury Coat

In 1811, however, Newbury made a plucky bid to regain its former fame in cloth making. Sir John Throckmorton of Buckland wagered 1,000 guineas that he would sit down to dinner at 8 p.m. wearing a coat made from wool which was still on the backs of the sheep at 5 a.m. that same morning. Mr. John Coxeter of the Greenham Mills had undertaken to weave the cloth and Mr. James White then cut the coat and had it made up. Sir John won his bet as the coat, which was damson coloured and which is still in existence, was ready by 6.20 p.m. The sheep were killed, roasted and distributed to the people, while Mr. Coxeter provided 120 gallons of strong ale to celebrate the event for which the town is famous.

Trade in the 19th Century

From the first years of the 19th century, the prosperity of Newbury grew apace, and the increase in trade was largely due to the canal connections with Reading and London, and with Bristol and the west. Many new industries had sprung up such as iron foundries, boatbuilding yards, and the gas works opened in 1825. The older industries, the corn and malt mills and the breweries continued to flourish, and only the cloth trade flagged.

Horse Racing

Horse racing has long been popular in Newbury. In the 18th century, the races took place on The Wash and in the early 19th century on Enborne Heath which is now enclosed. The present fine Racecourse which was opened in 1905, is one of the best in the country.

The Newbury Coat, worn by the grandson of John Coxeter, Mr. John James Coxeter, c1900.

The East Fields and West Fields at Newbury were enclosed in 1849, and The Wash in 1858.

Plenty's Lifeboat

In 1816, William Plenty invented a lifeboat which was launched at West Mills, and this was the forerunner of all modern lifeboats. Ten years before this, Plenty had invented an improved iron plough which remained the best plough in the kingdom for many years. His son, Edward, expanded the works and improved the lifeboat; and the works still flourish in new premises at Hambridge Road.

Machine Riots

Terrible scenes occurred in the neighbourhood during the Machine Riots in November, 1830. The farm labourers were demanding higher wages and less machinery, especially in regard to the new threshing machine, as this caused unemployment. They rioted, and supported by a mob of hooligans, marched on various farms, breaking up all farm machines, setting barns and ricks on fire and, in some cases, burning down the houses. A detachment of the Grenadier Guards was sent from London to help quell the riot and all the townsmen who could come mounted were told to assemble in the Market Place. They paraded at mid-day with the former Donnington Castle and Newbury Troop of Yeomanry. At Speenhamland they were joined by another company of horsemen which had assembled at the George and Pelican. Trotting to Gravel Hill at Stockcross they were strengthened by more mounted men, led by Lord Craven. They moved off along the Bath Road towards Kintbury, which was the centre of the disorder, with the Guards following in coaches. Another party under Col. Dundas and Capt. Houblon joined them at the Kintbury turning. The horsemen surrounded the village while the Guards and others searched the houses. The rioters were mostly found in the public-houses, and many arrests were made. Inkpen, West and East Woodhay, and Highclere were then searched; and altogether about a hundred men were taken into custody. Only one Berkshire man was executed, but many were transported or sent to prison.

The Railway

Newbury had always relied for its prosperity on the fact that important trade routes; East-West (London-Bristol) and North-South (the industrial midlands-Southampton) passed through the town. The advent of the railway was, therefore, watched with unease as it spelt disaster for both the canal companies and the coaching trade. The Great Western Railway completed its line between Bristol and London via Didcot and Swindon in 1841. From then on heavy goods that had previously travelled by canal between Bristol, Newbury and Reading and thence along the Thames to London could be carried by rail at half the cost and in hours rather than weeks, along a track that was not liable to freeze over in winter or dry up in summer.

Likewise the railway transformed the pattern of long distance passenger travel. The stage coaches could not compete in terms of speed, cost, and not least comfort. As each new section of line opened up so travellers switched to the train. The coaches were required to cover an ever diminishing portion of the route. The last stage coach between Bristol and London ran in 1843. Newbury, lying halfway between the two, felt the loss of its passing trade keenly. Many famous coaching inns closed and the large number of people they employed were put out of work. Without the revenue from coaches at their tolls, the turnpike trusts, which maintained the roads went bankrupt. Development and improvements in road surfacing were abandoned. The Bath Road lost its bustle and glamour and became once more a quiet country track, lying in peaceful neglect until the coming of the motor car at the end of the century.

The railway brought a new prosperity to the towns it linked. Reading, connected by rail to most parts of the country, grew quickly from a market town into a busy commercial and administrative centre. Newbury had been by-passed by these new arteries of communication. However, in 1847 a branch line from Reading to Newbury and Hungerford was opened, which was further extended to Trowbridge in the 1850's.

Later the Didcot, Newbury and Southampton Railway Company was formed to provide the vital North-South rail link. The G.W.R. agreed to operate the line when it was built. Work began in 1879. The Didcot to Newbury section opened in 1882, and Newbury to Winchester in 1885. The opening in April 1882 was marked by gigantic festivity in Newbury; the entire town was decked out in flags and flowers. The grand procession of dignitaries to the inaugural train included a detachment of the Royal Berkshire Yeomanry Cavalry, the band of the 93rd Sutherland Highlanders, and Newbury's Fire Brigade with engine and four white horses.

Newbury Station, c1905.

Although not the principal cause of the rejoicing, these celebrations coincided with the final agreement by the G.W.R. to improve facilities at Newbury Station. Before then there had simply been two very short platforms, with a shelter on the Up-line only, described by one unhappy passenger as 'an undersized chicken coop'. Following the improvements of 1882, the station was further altered in 1900 and then completely rebuilt between 1908 and 1910 as part of the upgrading of the line which had now become the major rail link to the West of England. The result is the building that stands today together with the present line layout consisting of four main tracks and three bays, two now disused.

A line was opened from Newbury to Lambourn in 1898. It was operated for seven years by the Lambourn Valley Railway Company before being taken over by the G.W.R.

During the first four decades of this century the railways became steadily less profitable as competition grew from the new generation of motor vehicles and roads. Finally, after intensive use during the Second World War, it became obvious in the 1950's that some of the lines running through Newbury would have to close. Passenger traffic on the Didcot-Newbury-Winchester line ceased in the early 1960's and in 1966 the line closed completely. Passenger traffic on the Lambourn line stopped in 1960 but the section between Newbury and Welford Park earned a reprieve until 1973 because of its proximity to the American Air Force munitions depot at Welford. A three mile stretch of line connected the base and Welford Park Station. Finally, this section too closed after a dispute as to the cost of repairs to bridges along the track. A final nostalgic train for enthusiasts was run on 3rd November, 1973.

Newbury was then left as a main line station only, with good services to London and the West Country, and connections for the north and south of England through Reading.

Later Events

Other principal events of the 19th century were: The building of the Corn Exchange in 1862; the foundation of the Newbury Field Club in 1870; the new Cattle Market in 1873; and the extension of the borough boundaries to include Speenhamland and other areas in 1878. Additions to the Town Hall were made in 1878, to include the Council Chamber and Magistrates' Court, the Clock Tower being completed in 1881. The Town Hall was demolished in 1908, when the present Municipal Offices were erected and the Mansion House Street widened.

The Twentieth Century

The Great Snowfall

1908 was the year of heavy snowfalls in the town. After a bitterly cold January, and then a bright but very dry February, March 4th saw the arrival of heavy snow which caused damage estimated at £500. Part of this was to telegraph and telephone lines and subscribers to the new service realised how much they had already begun to depend on it. The snow quickly thawed but the weather soon turned bitterly cold again, with gales and tempestuous rain.

Then, on Saturday, April 15th, the snow struck again with a fall lasting fifteen hours. The market closed early and local tradesmen one by one abandoned their deliveries in the face of the strong blizzard. It finally ceased on the Sunday morning and the big clearing up operation began. Several postcards were issued to commemorate the freak snowfall and they show many of Newbury's well-known landmarks white in heavy alpine splendour. There was however, much unemployment and hardship caused by the severe weather that winter and there were many requests for relief from the poor of the town.

The World Wars

Newbury sent its full quota of men and women on service in the World Wars of 1914-18 and 1939-45, and the names of those who made the supreme sacrifice have been engraved on bronze panels on the War Memorial. The names total nearly 300, and include civilian and Civil Defence personnel who lost their lives as a result of enemy action. Three Newbury firemen were killed when helping to fight the enemy blitz on Southampton. The Memorial occupies a prominent position on the north-east corner of St. Nicolas's Churchyard, in the centre of the town. During the war of 1939-45, air raid sirens in Newbury were sounded on 244 occasions, bringing the aggregate time spent under 'Alert' conditions to over 400 hours. On November 7th, 1940, bombs fell on Newbury without causing much damage, and on the same night 40 incendiaries were dropped, one falling on the north porch of the Parish Church. On March 26th, 1941, six H.E. bombs were dropped to fall on open ground, but houses and streets were machine gunned, damaging roofs and windows, and several people sustained slight cuts. There were two separate raids that day. On a Wednesday afternoon, February 10th, 1943, a hit-and-run raid by a single Dornier plane was a calamity to life and costly to property. Fifteen people were killed, including almsmen, women over 80 and children of tender age, while several others were injured. The bombs demolished Newbury Senior Council School opposite the railway station, St. John's Church, St. Bartholomew's Almshouses, and ten houses. Sixteen other houses were so badly damaged that demolition became necessary; 13 had to be evacuated and 294 houses, shops and other property received lesser damage, including broken windows.

A portion of Greenham Common was occupied by the 101st U.S.A. Airborne Division and planes with scores of gliders took off from here to take part in the invasion of Europe on D-Day, June 6th, 1944.

Greenham Common Airbase

After its partial use during the Second World War, there came a proposal from the Air Ministry in March 1951 to acquire most of Greenham and Crookham Common for conversion into a permanent heavy bomber base for the American Air Force. This met with great local opposition and well over 10,000 people of Newbury and district signed a petition against it. However, the airfield was constructed at a cost of over £8,000,000.

It was used as a base for B47 heavy bombers until 1968 since when it has become a standby base only, although it remains fully capable of instant conversion to full operational use. In 1978 the townspeople were furious when it was revealed that a proposal was being considered to make the airbase operational again for use by heavy inflight refuelling aircraft. The proposition was finally dropped after an outcry of public protest because of the airfield's proximity to what had become a heavy residential area. It now remains as a standby base only, but the biannual air tattoo brings large crowds to the airfield, and both the Air Force and local charities greatly benefit from the event.

The Racecourse at War

Newbury Racecourse played its part in the two World Wars. The course had been opened in 1905 after John Porter, the noted trainer, had enlisted the help of King Edward VII to persuade the Stewards of the Jockey Club to grant a license for a new racecourse. Mr. Lloyd H. Baxendale of Greenham, who owned the land, became Chairman of the company formed to finance the project. The first meeting attracted 15,000 spectators and a remarkable field of runners, and the success of the course was assured.

In the First World War it was occupied by the South Midlands Mounted Brigade at the outbreak of hostilities, but it was opened for racing in 1915. By 1916 it had become an inspection depot for the War Office, then a tank repair park, and a prisoner of war camp.

By 1919 racing was resumed and between the Wars improvements were made to both the course and the stands, making it one of the finest racecourses in the country.

On September 3rd, 1939, when war was again declared, the stands, stables, paddock, and car park were immediately requisitioned and

The Racecourse in Camp, 1915.

were soon occupied by troops. An R.A.S.C. main supply depot was installed east of the stands but, in spite of difficulties, racing continued during 1940 and 1941. However, in 1942 it became a marshalling yard for the American Army and all racing ceased. Sidings were laid on the straight mile, petrol stores including a major part of the oil for the North African landings were on the course, and later Bailey bridging, landing nets, hutments, and other equipment arrived in readiness for the invasion of Europe. Thick coconut matting, covered with loads of soil and ashes, was used to cover the course as a protection. In 1945, after the Normandy landings had caused most of the stores to be removed, an experimental clearing began to see what damage had been done; but the difficulties were not over. Prisoners of war occupied the stable block, and in March 1946 the Ministry of Supply arrived with more and more stores. It was not until 2nd July, 1947 that the centre of the course was released. By this time the damage was extensive, but sheer hard work and time healed the scars and on 1st April, 1949 racing was resumed.

Happily, the course is now in perfect condition again. Members of the Royal Family frequently attend to see such important races as the Hennessy Gold Cup.

Education

Friday, May 26th, 1972 was an important date in Newbury's history for it was the occasion of a royal visit to the borough. H.M. Queen Elizabeth II walked through the Market Place and talked with the townspeople in a way which would have been deemed impossible by her more formal ancestors. It was the quincentenary of the founding of St. Bartholomew's Grammar School which brought this honour to the town. After being greeted at Newbury Racecourse Station by the Hon. David Smith, Lord Lieutenant of Berkshire, the Queen drove to Cheap Street where she was met by the Mayor of Newbury.

During her visit to the Grammar School she saw various school activities and a series of exhibits including a model illustrating the geology and wild life of the Berkshire Downs.

Since then changes have taken place. The school has now become a comprehensive together with the County Girls' Grammar School which was founded in 1909. They are known as St. Bartholomew's School.

Three more comprehensive schools, Park House, Shaw House, and Turnpike School also cater for the older children of Newbury while the younger members of the community are educated in primary and junior schools around the town. Adult education is provided by the Newbury College of Further Education.

Private schools also play their part, and one school, St. Gabriels, is housed in the historic Sandleford Priory where Mrs. Montagu entertained her learned and distinguished friends.

Hospitals

The Newbury and District Hospital, which is in the Andover Road, was built in 1885. It was remodelled and enlarged after 1918 at a cost of about £37,000. It possesses an operating theatre, X-ray room, private wards, and separate general wards for men, women, and children. Wireless is installed with headphones for every bed. Sandleford Hospital, in the Newtown Road, standing on high ground overlooking the town, cares for maternity and geriatric patients.

Parks and Open Spaces

In spite of the loss of most of Greenham Common's 856 acres which had been acquired by the Newbury Corporation prior to the takeover by the Air Ministry, few towns can claim as many acres of parks and public open spaces as Newbury.

Victoria Park has an area of some 17 acres. With its model boating lake and children's playground, tennis courts, putting green and bowling green, and bandstand enclosure surrounded with bright flower beds, it forms a valuable 'lung' in the centre of the town.

Greenham House grounds form a smaller, pleasant retreat for townspeople.

There is the large City Recreation Ground, and another one at Wash Common. Stroud Green, purchased by the Corporation in 1938, Goldwell Park, and Northcroft bring the total up to about 90 acres.

Northcroft is now the venue for the Michaelmas Fair, held on the Thursday following October 11th. Originally the occasion for hiring farm labourers, it was held in the town centre until 1946.

Queen Victoria's Statue

It was in Sandleford Park that George Sanger, a Newbury boy, captured two hares which were to form part of an act with which he toured the country. It was the humble beginning of his Great Circus that brought him fame and fortune. But he always remembered the place of his birth.

Early in the century he presented a statue of Queen Victoria to the town. It was made by Messrs. Doulton and Company of the Royal Doulton Potteries at Lambeth, and was inscribed 'To the Great and Good Queen Victoria, 1819-1901.' George Sanger's daughter, Mrs. Reeve, unveiled the statue on Wednesday, 24th June, 1903. It stood in the Market Place, protected by four terra cotta lions, until it became a hazard to the ever increasing traffic. In 1933 it was removed to Greenham House grounds and finally, with only two lions in attendance, it was taken to Victoria Park, where it stands today.

Museum and Library

Another tribute was paid to Queen Victoria when the old Cloth Hall was restored in her memory and presented to the Corporation, who decided to use it as a Museum.

In 1906 the Carnegie Public Library was opened thus providing a source of knowledge and entertainment to thousands of readers. Both the Museum and the Library are described in the chapter 'The Architectural Heritage'.

Newbury Weekly News

The Newbury Weekly News, first published in 1867, faithfully reports on local events, both in Newbury and the surrounding villages. It has been adjudged the model of what a country town newspaper should be and now has a circulation of 27,000 copies weekly.

The Arts

The town has been fortunate in having fine musicians living nearby to foster an interest in choral and orchestral societies and to establish the annual Newbury Music Festival. The Newbury Symphony Orchestra, formerly the Newbury Amateur Orchestral Union, is believed to be the oldest full amateur symphony orchestra in the country. It was founded over 90 years ago. These societies, together with operatic and dramatic societies, ensure entertainment for Newburians throughout the year.

The Newbury Art Group stages a summer exhibition of the work of local artists, and the Camera Club has a show in the spring. The Gramophone Society, the Newbury Fine Art Group, and the Literary Society attract members from the town and the surrounding district. The Newbury Arts Festival held in June 1978 fulfilled its purpose by preparing the way for the opening of the new Arts Workshop and by spreading enjoyment of the arts and creating a wider knowledge of local activities. H.R.H. The Duchess of Kent attended the Gala Concert which opened the ten-day programme of music, drama, and ballet. This has now become a successful annual event.

Newbury Arts Workshop

This was opened by the President, Lady Porchester, in October 1978. Much fund raising and hard work by a dedicated band of people had transformed the old Temperance Hall in Northcroft Lane into a modern arts workshop. Courses and lectures are arranged to stimulate an interest in the arts, and clubs and groups can use the hall for their meetings.

The Waterside Youth Centre

The Waterside Youth Centre on the site of the old Waterside Chapel on the banks of the River Kennet, was completed in 1964 at a cost of £42,000. It is built on the open plan system and a gallery on the first floor is linked to an open veranda and balcony overlooking the river. The County Youth Service provides a wide range of activities here for young people between the ages of 14 and 20.

Also to be found in Newbury are other organisations such as Scouts, Guides, Cadets, boys' and girls' mixed clubs, and specialist clubs. A complete list and further information may be obtained from the Youth and Community Officer for the Newbury District, Pelican Lane, Newbury. Telephone 43115.

One of the oldest societies, the Newbury Field Club, was founded in 1870 and is still very active. Its members enjoy lectures on archaeological, architectural, and historical subjects, and on natural history, and during the summer months excursions are arranged to many places of interest.

Swimming Pool

The swimming pool in Northcroft is 240 ft. long by 40 ft. wide. It was first built over 80 years ago but was completely modernised in 1937, when a plant was put in to chlorinate, filter, and circulate the water. The pool was then altered to have a deep and shallow end and further improvements were carried out in 1963, including a children's paddling pool and lido.

Fair Close Day Centre

The Fair Close Day Centre was opened in 1967 by H.M. Queen Elizabeth the Queen Mother. It is a godsend to many retired people who come regularly for a hot meal and companionship. Some live in the adjacent modern flats. The 'Meals on Wheels' service is also run from the centre's modern kitchen.

Divisional Police Headquarters and Court Buildings

These buildings in Mill Lane were completed in 1965, costing £192,550. Adjacent to the Police Station is the Magistrates' Court which includes a Juvenile Court. Also held in the building are Crown Courts, County Courts, sittings of the Tax Commissioner, the Rating and Valuation Panel, and the Coroner's Court.

The Traffic Problem

Newbury is situated at the crossing point of two major trunk roads, the A4 and the A34. During the 1950's and the 1960's the town centre became more and more congested as an increasing volume of cars and heavy lorries pressed their way through streets designed for carriages rather than juggernauts. The first relief road, Western Avenue, was constructed in the late fifties and routed A4 traffic away from the Broadway. The opening of the M4 in December 1971 then took long distance traffic off the A4 altogether. The ring road by-pass (completed in 1966) freed Northbrook Street from a continuous and noisy queue of North-South A34 traffic. Finally, the Sandleford Link, opened in 1979, ended a bottleneck south of the town and allowed through traffic to by-pass the centre of Newbury completely on a dual carriageway road.

Newbury Today

Newbury today is a busy and prosperous town. Thankfully, too it is still one of great elegance and beauty. Its largely eighteenth century centre has been spared the type of comprehensive modernization scheme which has altered the character of so many English towns. However, modernization there has been.

Demands of modern businesses have produced office blocks,

supermarkets, a new telephone exchange, and a large new shopping complex that incorporates the bus station and a multi-story car park. New shop fronts have been fitted to most houses in the main streets of the town centre; some sympathetically, others not.

The erection of new buildings has meant the demolition of many older ones of historic and architectural merit. During the 1970's at least twenty-seven in this category disappeared.

It is hoped that in the coming decades, a sensible balance can be struck between what has to be changed in order to keep the town efficient in business and shopping terms, and what should be left alone if Newbury is to preserve its historic character and remain a pleasant place in which people can enjoy living.

The Architectural Heritage

The short description of the streets and roads of Newbury in the following pages will give some idea of the principal buildings which have not yet been described. Some historic buildings that have been demolished in recent years have been included in the hope that their past features of interest will not be forgotten. The streets are followed generally from North to South and those who wish to use the description as a basis for a tour of the town will find the map on pages 6 and 7 useful. The map is based on the eighteenth century plan of Newbury but modern streets have been superimposed.

Periods allotted to buildings should be taken as only approximate unless a definite date appears on the buildings in question or in records.

Where buildings are occupied by shops, they are described under the names of the shops on the ground floor, and not by street numbers which are often hard to find if they are there. In a number of cases, two or more shops occupy one building, and are therefore described together.

It has been attempted to describe all buildings dating from before 1750, that is up to the Early Georgian period, with a few later buildings of special architectural or historical interest. Newbury is rich in Mid- and Late-Georgian buildings and also Regency houses; but space does not allow for a complete description of these.

Periods

The following architectural periods are used in the description.

(1) Medieval to 1485. Early Tudor, 1485 - 1547. Late Tudor, 1547 - 1603.

(2) Jacobean, Charles I and Commonwealth, 1603 - 1660. Charles II, 1660 - 1685.

(3) James II - William and Mary, 1685 - 1702. Queen Anne, 1702 - 1714.

(4) Early Georgian, 1714 - 1750. Mid-Georgian, 1750 - 1790.

(5) Late Georgian, 1790 - 1810. Regency, 1810 - 1830. Modern after 1830.

SPEENHAMLAND

Speenhamland is that part of Newbury which lies on the north side of the North Brook. This stream ran from the pond on the west side of the Albert Works, then north of Barclays Bank and crossing Northbrook Street, it ran to The Marsh (Victoria Park).

BATH ROAD

Castle Houses

Starting from Castle Houses on the Bath Road and off the west side of the plan; this was formerly the famous Castle Inn. It is a large building of three storeys; the western part being Early Georgian and the eastern part Mid-Georgian. The building underwent considerable alterations when it was converted into three houses in the 19th century. The Lawn has a good Early Georgian front, but the remainder of the building has been rebuilt.

Northbrook Street from the Bridge, 1851.

Goldwell

Beyond and opposite on the south side of the road, is Goldwell, a large house dating from the Early Georgian period and said to have been built about 1740; but the fine staircase appears to be in an earlier style. The house has been converted into offices and a small housing estate has been built in the grounds. The adjoining Goldwell Park is a pleasant public park.

Speen Court

Speen Court (Southern Electricity Board) appears on the west side of the plan. This is a lovely Mid-Georgian house, and the variegated brick walls are ornamented with brick pilasters and a moulded cornice. The large bow window is a Regency addition, and there are later extensions on the north side of the house.

"The Chestnuts"

Beyond stands "The Chestnuts", one of the most beautiful houses of the very early Georgian period. The date 1720 appears on the roof, but the building is more in the Queen Anne style. It is built of variegated brick and is of two storeys with attic dormer windows on the tiled roof. The south front has a pediment and the front doorway has decorations of the period. The large bow window on the west side is a Regency addition. The house, which contains a fine staircase of the early 18th century and some good panelling, has recently been completely restored, and is now used as offices by Hymac Ltd.

Oxford Road

No. 20 is of the Mid-Georgian period but has been restored and converted into offices. The original doorway and fanlight have been retained.

PELICAN LANE

Pelican Lane has several old cottages and it runs past the old Police Station, now Health Departments, to the Farm where there are some old cottages and a barn.

Speenhamland Lane forms a connection with London Road.

OXFORD STREET

This street, with the Broadway and the west part of London Road, was the busiest part of Speenhamland, and the important and popular coaching centre from the 17th century until the opening of the railway. Being almost midway between London and Bath, 34 or more coaches would arrive daily and numbers of passengers would alight and stay in the great inns here. There are several Mid- to Late-Georgian houses in Oxford Street and, near the west and on the south side, No. 35 and 35a are an interesting pair. They appear to be of the Charles II period, and their doorways, high above the roadway, are approached by a flight of steps, with curious stone openings to the basement. They are of three storeys and of mellow red brick with a beautifully moulded cornice.

Old Theatre

Two narrow alleyways used to lead from the north side of Oxford Street to a small open space in front of the old theatre which has now been demolished. The theatre, which was built in 1802, contained a painted ceiling said to be unique in the theatres of the period. Here many famous actors and actresses performed before the rich and distinguished visitors staying at Speenhamland. A coloured print of it can be seen in the Museum.

Beyond are two of the old inns which still flourish as modern hotels.

Bacon Arms

The Bacon Arms has been modernised but the ground floor rooms retain some old beams supporting the ceilings and are said to date from the 17th century.

The Chequers

The Chequers has been rebuilt almost entirely, but some old walling remains. There is also a timber-framed wall on the east side, and this is part of an old malthouse which is partly of the 17th century. No. 4, next door, is a three-storey red-brick house of the Early- Mid-Georgian period with a good doorway.

THE BROADWAY

There was formerly a wayside chapel at The Broadway, where the clock and octagonal shelter now form a round-about for traffic. The chapel was disused in the 16th century and converted into houses which were demolished in 1791. On the north side, La Riviera and Cooper's were formerly the Bear Inn, an Early-Mid Georgian building of variegated brick. There is some early panelling in one of the upper rooms, and at the back is the old brewery, now used for storage.

York House

York House, now Lloyds Bank, is one of the most notable buildings in the town and is of the Queen Anne period or earlier. It is a three-storeyed red brick building with a bracketed cornice. The front is enriched by three pilasters and the windows are surmounted by alternate triangular and arched pediments. The house contains a contemporary staircase and some good panelling. Nos. 18 and 16 have late Georgian stucco fronts, but part of the buildings behind may be of the 17th century.

No. 19, Adams

On the south-west side of The Broadway facing the clock-tower, this house is Mid-Georgian with delightful slightly bowed shop windows. Lower down, Nos. 5 to 9 (Woodhead's, Newbury Laundry, etc.), have Late Georgian fronts to brick and timber houses which are probably of the Queen Anne period. There are several Mid-Late Georgian buildings on this side, although a few have been replaced by modern buildings.

The King's Coffee House

Opposite, The King's Coffee House may date from the William and Mary period, but it has been much altered and the front was rebuilt in the 19th century. It is now occupied by Pearsons, the estate agents.

LONDON ROAD

The George and Pelican

Round the corner, in the narrow part of the London Road, is the Pelican Yard. The George and Pelican was, perhaps, the most famous of the Speenhamland inns, and Quin's oft-quoted lines are still remembered:

"The famous inn at Speenhamland,
That stands below the hill,
May well be called 'The Pelican',
From its enormous bill."

The Yard is now scheduled for redevelopment.

Cross Keys

The Cross Keys was another of the large posting inns which was rebuilt in the 19th century. Nos. 5 and 7, and the adjoining shop, on the south side, are Early-Mid Georgian with a stucco front; and the three hipped roofs on gables can be seen from the yard behind. Beyond the passageway is a building, formerly the Phoenix Inn, mainly Early Georgian, containing a fine contemporary staircase with turned balusters and a moulded handrail. Some redevelopment is taking place in this area.

Elizabeth Cottage

Elizabeth Cottage (c. 1800), to the rear of Smith's bakehouse, has an heraldically painted ceiling unique in the town, with carved cornice and decorated chimney pieces; probably once a single storey building and used as a retreat from the turmoil of the adjacent coaching inns. At present it is undergoing extensive renovation.

Spring's

Spring's Cafe is of the Queen Anne period or earlier, with

The Broadway and Northbrook Street, facing south.

The Broadway, facing London Road, c1905.

cemented walls. There is a tile-hung gable at the back and there are two large chimney stacks. The house contains one of the finest staircases in the town with twisted balusters and beautifully moulded handrail of about 1700, painted white. Opposite are Mid-Georgian houses and shops, some of which are being replaced by modern offices.

Manor House, Pitman & Bazett

Facing Park Way, is No. 34, the Manor House which is of two storeys with an Early Georgian stuccoed front, a moulded cornice, and three attic dormer windows in the tiled roof. The building behind may date from the Charles II period or earlier and there are two gabled projections at the back. The staircase is of the 17th century and has renewed balusters. No. 40 has a late Georgian grey brick front with Gothic windows, on the Mid Georgian House.

No. 44, John D. Wood

This is a good Georgian building, with the date 1750 or '59 on one of the bricks. It was built as a western extension of the Dower House, formerly the famous King's Arms Inn, a fine building in the Queen Anne style which, owing to dilapidation, was demolished a few years ago. Dick Turpin is said to have hidden at one time in the roof of a low projection at the back.

St. Joseph's Church

The Roman Catholic Church of St. Joseph is modern. It is built in the Italian basilican style with a detached campanile. From here to Thatcham Gate, the London Road is comparatively modern. Beyond the disused railway the road is quite new, where it by-passes the former loop which ran by Ham Manor.

Millwaters

To the north is Millwaters, a picturesque Early Georgian house with later extensions at the back. It is of red brick and of two storeys with two attic dormer windows in the brown tiled roof.

Hambridge Farm

To the south-east is Hambridge Farm which has a 17th century house built of flint and brick with a central chimney stack. It is partly tile-hung and retains its old casement windows with leaded lights. The large barn is of the same period, but has been put to modern usage by Hambridge Frozen Foods.

SHAW ROAD

Shaw Road was the old highway to London. Shaw (formerly Smith's) Crescent, consists mainly of Regency houses. Shaw Bridge House retains some features of interest and is said to have been standing when the Second Battle of Newbury was fought. It has been considerably altered since then; but some of the old timber-framing can be seen inside and there is a tile-hung gable. The staircase may be Georgian.

NORTHBROOK STREET

Northbrook Street begins on the south side of the North Brook. It is the finest street in Newbury, one of the most picturesque streets in the country.

No. 50

An alleyway leads by the side of No. 50 where, on the side wall of

Northbrook Street from the Bridge, c1903.

the brick and timber building there is a long weavers' window. This shop is probably of the Charles II period, and the building above the shop is tile-hung with three attic dormer windows in the tiled roof. The shops on the opposite side of the street are Mid-Late Georgian.

Monument Inn

The Monument Inn appears to be early Jacobean and is of two storeys with two tile-hung gables. The front is stuccoed and painted and there is a Georgian extension at the back. Old oak beams support the ceilings inside. Standing back beyond the inn is a Methodist Church.

No. 42. Vision Hire

Opposite are some Mid-Late Georgian houses above shops and then No. 42. This is one of the most notable buildings in Newbury and the front above the shops is divided into three sections by Corinthian pilasters, the middle section being about twice the width of those at the sides. In each section is a large window with a semi-circular head, and the keystones are carved with figures of small children. The middle window has two Ionic pilasters on each side supporting a richly moulded entablature. There are some initials on the left, and the date 1724 on the right. A modillioned entablature is supported by the four Corinthian pilasters, and above are four pilasters, two supporting the arched pediment in the middle and one at each end of the side panels. There is another semi-circular headed window in the middle; and four figures representing the Seasons used to crown the front. It has been suggested that this building is very foreign in style and was possibly built by someone who had come from the Netherlands during Marlborough's wars which had ended a few years before. Lower down on the same side, 39a is a red brick three-storey building of the Early Georgian period.

No. 61

Davies' on the corner of West Street is a 16th century building with a Georgian stucco front and there is a good panelling and a staircase. Maynards' and the Tea Bar have a 19th century front, but the buildings beyond have a steep pitched roof and are possibly of the Charles II period. Lawrence's appears to be slightly later than the last, and has a stucco front. A wide passage which has beams supporting the ceiling of the room above leads to the Tandoori Restaurant and other buildings, and it is tile-hung at the back. No. 80 has a stucco front with a tile-hung gable and may be of the Queen Anne period. A wide passage leads to Cromwell Place which has Mid-Georgian houses. Beyond is the Congregational Church. Old buildings of the Charles II period to the south of Cromwell Place, have been demolished and replaced by modern shops.

Nos. 33 and 34

On the east side, The Newbury Weekly News, Olivers Shoes, and A. Jones and Sons, opposite West Street, share a late Georgian front with Venetian windows, and the building behind is older.

Nos. 28 and 29 are probably of the Queen Anne period with later stucco fronts. No. 26, at one time a Chapel, has a Mid Georgian front with two pilasters and a pediment, and the house behind is older with a hipped tile roof. Paige's and Manfield's are Jack of Newbury's House, described on p. 31. Marks and Spencers stands on the site of the old Jack of Newbury Inn. No. 16 and Woolworth's had interesting Early Georgian brick fronts above the shop level but these have been remodelled.

Camp Hopson's

The northern part of Camp Hopson's range is Mid Georgian, and has two storeys of variegated brick above the shop front, each with five windows. There is a moulded cornice and large pediment. Next to this is one of the most notable and beautiful town buildings in England, and one of the earliest examples of rubbed brickwork. It is of the Charles II period, and dated 1669. Each of the two storeys above the shop has four windows and the front is ornamented with Doric and Ionic pilasters. There is a modillioned cornice, and the front is crowned by two tile-hung gables with windows to the top floor under the tiled roof. There are similar pairs of gables at the sides, and one gable at the back where there is also a gabled stairway enclosed by buildings. The fine staircase has a plaster ceiling ornamented with a cherub medallion. The next building stands back a little, and is Mid-Late Georgian. It is of variegated brick with a moulded cornice and parapet. The first storey has eight windows and the second storey five.

Nos. 91 and 92

Hilton and Freeman Hardy & Willis is a fine Mid Georgian building with a rubbed brick front with eight tall pilasters, a moulded cornice and parapet. It is of three storeys, and some of the pilasters have been cut away on the ground floor for the shop fronts. The house was probably built by one of the Head family and a gutter head is dated 1774. Wm. G. Corke & Son appears to date from the Charles II period, but the stucco front is Late Georgian. The middle blind window of the first floor has a bracketed pediment. The Anchor Inn has a stucco front and side but the core and roof are possibly Tudor.

Golden Egg Restaurant

Milward's and the Golden Egg Restaurant were formerly one building and appear to date from the late Tudor period. The front is stuccoed over old timber-framing and the building has been much re-modelled. The top storey was originally composed of three gable windows whose form can be seen from the inside. Heavy oak beams support the ceilings of the Cafe on the ground floor and first floor. Toomer's, opposite, stands on the site of the old Rose and Crown Inn which dated from the Tudor period.

Old Rectory

A path leads down east to the riverside and (now incorporated in

POUND STREET

On the other side of the railway bridge, No. 62, formerly The Black Boys, and the buildings beyond and round the corner into Pound Street are Mid-Late Georgian. Garden House is Mid Georgian and has a richly-moulded brick cornice in front which appears to be earlier. Opposite, on the corner of Argyle Road, Bartholomew Close is of one storey with two tile-hung gables, and may date from the Queen Anne period. But it has been much restored and the windows are modern.

ARGYLE ROAD

St. Bartholomew's Hospital in Argyle Road has been described on p. 24.

Bartholomew Manor

Opposite is Bartholomew Manor which is believed to stand on the site of the old manor house of Newbury and, under its earlier name, Ulvritone. But it apparently became reduced to the status of a farm house, possibly in the second half of the 15th century when it came into the king's hands; and in 1518 it is described as a barn and close, and between 1535 and 1579 as Bartholomew Farm. The house was leased to Jack of Newbury in 1518, but he died in the following year. The house is certainly medieval and may date from the 14th to early 15th century, but has been altered considerably in later periods. The north gable and chimney stack, and the stack in the middle of the house, are early Tudor. There are later additions at the back. The house contains two Tudor fireplaces, remains of the old staircase, and panelling and a fireplace of the early 18th century. A full description of the house is given in Transactions of the Newbury Field Club, VI, No. 3; and this includes a description of the next buildings.

Nurses' Homes

These were formerly known as "Raymonds", and it has been suggested that a large medieval timber farm building was converted into a house in the 16th. century. It was remodelled as Raymond's Almshouses before 1676; but these were abandoned when the later almshouses were built. Dr. Essex Wynter converted the building into homes for the retired nurses. The homes form a most picturesque group and consist of a long building with a gabled porch in the middle, and wings at each end extending to the road. The buildings are timber-framed and of two storeys with gabled attic dormer windows and two gables at the back. Over the porch are the arms of the Brewers' Company, dated 1670. To the south are the new Nurses' Homes, a delightful modern building with a picturesque porch; and opposite are the Upper Raymond's Almshouses which were built in 1826. There are several Mid-Late Georgian cottages in The City, and a small Mission Hall.

NEWTOWN ROAD

The Litten Chapel has been described on p. 25, and opposite are the Lower Raymond's Almshouses which were built in 1796. Another group of almshouses here was destroyed by enemy action in 1943. On the site has been built a day centre for old people known as "Fair Close" together with a block of flats. The new Church of St. John stands on the site of the destroyed building on the corner of St. John's Road. Further south are St. John's Infant School, the Church Almshouses, and the Old Cemetery. This cemetery was started by a private company in 1847. The Corporation acquired the cemetery by Act of Parliament 1953. The town's New Cemetery is situated north of the borough off the Hermitage Road.

ANDOVER ROAD AND WASH COMMON

The Andover Road leads by the Newbury District Hospital and St. Bartholomew's School (formerly the County Girls' Grammar School) and at the top of the hill is the Falkland Memorial. p. 39.

Essex Street leads by Falkland Garth to the site of the First Battle of Newbury, p. 37, and the Burial Mounds, p. 40. On the west side of the Andover Road stands the picturesque Church of St. George, built in 1933 in the early Italian style. Now that it has been completed, with a campanile attached by a cloister to the nave, it is one of the most beautiful modern churches in Berkshire. On the east side is Park House Comprehensive School. Further south, the River Enborne forms the boundary between Newbury and Hampshire.

MANSION HOUSE STREET

The buildings on the north side of Mansion House Street are all of three storeys, Beynon's is a brick Mid Georgian building with moulded brickwork around the windows. The back rooms are on a

Market Square, with Queen Victoria's statue, c1904.

different level and considerably earlier, possibly Charles II; and behind these, backing on to the river is a Mid Georgian two-storey building. The lower room was formerly a large bake-house and over is a large high room with two bay windows overlooking the river. This was the chief room of the Guildhall Coffee House which formerly occupied the building which had at a still earlier date been an inn. The Halifax Building Society's offices next door, are Early Georgian. The front is of red brick and the windows have curved lintels. There is a range of Mid Georgian out-buildings at the back. Parts of most of the above buildings are probably of the Tudor period.

MARKET PLACE

The next buildings to the east are Beynon's and face the Market Place. This was formerly two houses, Nos. 34 and 32, and they have Mid-Late Georgian brick fronts. No. 32 had two bay windows on the first floor until recently, and behind the front rooms this house is earlier and may date from Charles II period. There is a fine staircase of about 1700 from the first to the second floor with twisted balusters and a moulded handrail. There is another old building by the riverside with a timber-framed gable. This shop was established in 1827, and in those early days the lady shoppers used to be given a glass of wine, the men a glass of ale. On the other side of the modern bank is The Old Waggon and Horses, one of the oldest inns in the town. The front is stuccoed and this may conceal half-timbering. The timber-framing was formerly exposed at the side and the back; and the building probably dates from the Jacobean period. The upper part of the staircase has square newels and massive turned balusters of the early 17th century. A long room extends back to the river on the first floor and has heavy beams with queen posts; and the front bar has a chamfered beam supporting the ceiling.

WHARF STREET

The offices of Day, Shergold & Herbert on the north side of Wharf Street have a stucco front; but the building is partly timber-framed and may date from the Charles II period. The first floor overhangs on the west side with renewed tile-hanging, and the inside of the building has been re-modelled. The offices of Louch, Belcher & Co. next door have a striking three-storeyed red brick front in the Queen Anne style; and the date on one of the bricks of the front was probably scratched many years after they were built. The entrance hall has lovely panelling with fluted pilasters to the passage leading to the stairway, all of the early 18th century. The beautiful staircase has turned balusters alternately fluted with a moulded handrail and delicately carved brackets at each step. There is old panelling in the upper rooms. The wing at the back was added later in the 18th century and the large room on the first floor has two good Adam-style doorways, a Corinthian Venetian window, and a moulded plaster frieze. The old stables to the east have been demolished and part of the restored offices converted into the Wharf Street Hall. Opposite and facing the Market Place is No. 24 Market Place, formerly The White Hart Hotel. The front part is of three storeys and partly timber-framed, covered with stucco. The building appears to date from the 16th century, and an old window frame removed from one of the bottom rooms on Wharf Street is said to have been inscribed 1516. The top floor was probably added in the late 17th century, and at this floor level there is a moulded cornice on the north side. Three of the windows above this have mullions and

The Museum.

transoms and are of three lights, the centre lights having semi-circular heads. Two of these windows are now walled up inside, and the fourth, eastern one, has been modernised. The two-storeyed east wing was probably added in the late 17th century, and the roof partly conceals the tile-hung gable of the older building. The ground and first floor windows of the front on the Market Place have slightly bowed windows of the Late Georgian period, and the two main doorways have side pilasters, fan-lights, and hoods.

The Museum

The Museum, formerly the Cloth Hall, is a beautiful Jacobean building of three storeys. The first floor overhangs on the north and west sides, and the lower wall on the north side is divided into six bays by wooden pillars with carved brackets supporting the moulded cornice. The restored west doorway has similar pillars and brackets supporting an overhanging porch. There is a west gable and three gables on the north side with windows to the attic floor, and the timber-framed walls above the first floor level are stuccoed. All the windows are mullioned. The building was restored in 1829 and 1897. In 1902 it was purchased, through the instrumentality of John Rankin, by a Committee who again restored it in memory of Queen Victoria, and it was handed to the Corporation who decided to use it as a Museum.

The exhibits illustrate the antiquities of the Newbury district. The lower galleries are devoted to a comprehensive series of exhibits illustrating the prehistoric background of the region. The upper galleries are devoted to the history and antiquities of Newbury from medieval times to the present day, and to Local Natural History, with an excellent collection of Moths and Butterflies. Special features of the Local History Gallery are a case devoted to the history of the famous Newbury Coat; a section setting out the history of the ancient parish of Shaw and its fine Elizabethan mansion; and the old documents and effects of the Newbury Company of Weavers, which was founded in the early 17th century. A particularly interesting section is devoted to the Battles of Newbury, illustrated by models in relief.

The Corn Stores

The Corn Stores, or Old Granary, stretches to the east of the Museum. It is a long and most picturesque galleried building of two storeys. The ground floor, now part of the Museum, is sheltered by the wide over-hanging gallery which is approached by two flights of stairs. The building possibly dates from the Charles II period, and is one of the few remaining buildings of this type in England.

Kendrick House is an Early-Mid Georgian building with later alterations and with a good front doorway with a fanlight.

Castle Site

To the east is the site of the Castle. The "Stone Building" probably occupies a part of the site; it is possibly built from the stone of the ruined Castle.

WHARF ROAD

This road was remodelled when the new Ring Road was constructed to the east of it and the Car Park, partly on the site of the old wet dock of the Newbury and Reading Canal of 1714, was laid out. This entailed the destruction of the medieval stone boundary wall of the Greenham Preceptory of Knights Hospitalers, and of the old galleried Store House which had stood by the dock.

The Granaries, Wharf Street.

MARKET PLACE

The Municipal Buildings are modern buildings with a high clock tower, fronting on Mansion House Street and the west side of the Market Place.

No. 27, now part of the Municipal Buildings, occupies two houses, dating from the Regency and Mid Georgian periods. Next to the last is an arcade leading to Bartholomew Street. During recent restorations, Daniels' uncovered walls of Queen Anne period and a lead plaque "1681", which has been inserted on an outside wall. The fronts above the shops to the south of this are Mid-Late Georgian; but the buildings behind No. 21 are partly Elizabethan and partly Queen Anne with Victorian windows on the ground floor, so that three English Queens are represented. From the passage-way can be seen the old windows and a moulded brick over-hanging, and there are three gables with remains of moulded bargeboards and pendants. Maynard's and Thresher's has a late Georgian front, but the building behind is earlier and from the back can be seen traces of timber-framing and Tudor bricks.

Two houses which until recent years stood opposite Black Bear Lane were formerly part of the Old King's Head Inn of 1643. The front was late Georgian but the building behind was earlier than the Inn and of the Tudor period. It was timber-framed with four gables at the back. The adjoining building had an exquisite 16th century ceiling divided into panels by heavy moulded and enriched beams with Tudor vine leaf panels in the angles, and supported in one place by a handwrought stanchion of iron. At the back of the building was a huge stone slab about 11 ft. long with a smooth surface and rounded corners. It is thought that this was used for rolling the bow strings for archers. (Transactions Newbury Field Club vii p.84). This stone is now by the Parish Church.

The Plaza

A little to the south of the White Hart, p. 84, an arcade leads to the Plaza Theatre, which was built in 1925. It was used by the local dramatic societies for their productions, and for other town functions. It is now a Club.

Hatchet Hotel

The Hatchet Hotel is mainly Late Georgian, and is dated at the back, 1807. A passage leads to a Mid Georgian cottage behind, and north of this passage the hotel is tile-hung at the back and possibly of this earlier period.

Corn Exchange

The Corn Exchange, dated 1862, is ornamented with classical pilasters, and its projecting front gives an air of distinction to the south end of the Market Place and is rather reminiscent of a 17th century Italian church.

Queen's Hotel

The Queen's Hotel dates mainly from the 19th century but some of the buildings at the back are earlier.

CHEAP STREET

Penn's has been rebuilt, but the old appearance was retained with three picturesque tile-hung gables in front. They have restored bargeboards and pendants, and are dated 1679 with the initials "S.A.M." Opposite were Kimber's Almshouses, built in 1795, now part of the Post Office – the almshouses being rebuilt in Kennet Road, in which are incorporated the old entrance gates and the inscription tablet.

On the west side of Cheap Street, all the old buildings between No. 33 Penn's and Market Street have now been pulled down to be replaced by the eastern part of the new shopping centre. A few of the demolished buildings dated from the sixteenth to eighteenth century. They included an ancient bake-house and a fine Queen Anne house, standing back with an earlier room to the west. In this room Lord Falkland is said to have spent the night and to have received Holy Communion early in the morning before the First Battle of Newbury. Excavations in this area revealed several old flint wells, indicating probably Saxon habitation.

No. 48, Kitchen and Bedroom Design, on the east side, has a grey brick early Georgian front, but parts of the building behind appear to be of the William and Mary period. There is a lovely staircase of about 1700 with square newels and twisted balusters; and a large back room on the first floor has good Mid Georgian panelling. The Welcome Cafe and No. 78 has a striking stucco front with a very deep coved cornice. The date 1637 is painted on the front and the building behind appears to be of this period. Number 53 has a late Georgian front to an earlier building. " The Lemon Plaice " has a tile-hung front and the building is probably Early Georgian. St. Mary's Almshouses were already considered ancient in 1604; but they were rebuilt in 1864 and have now been demolished. This southern end of Cheap Street was formerly called St. Mary's Hill.

Public Library

The Public Library, which was built in 1905-6 with a grant from the Carnegie Trust Fund and was enlarged and modernised in 1968, stands near the site of a 17th century workhouse which was called "The Gaol". A large beam from the old building is incorporated in the library gable. In 1974 the library ceased to be the Newbury Public Library, under the jurisdiction of the Borough, and became a branch of the Berkshire County Library. Further alterations were made to the building to modernise the reference library, the reading room, and gramophone record library. A separate room was provided for the study of local history. In 1966 there were 35,000 books on the shelves. The number had increased to 50,000 by 1972, and by 1979 to nearly 65,000. As a divisional library it handles a total of 87,000 books to cater for the needs of Newbury, Thatcham, Hungerford, Lambourn, and the West Berkshire Mobile libraries.

Neate's

Neate's offices has a Late Georgian variegated brick front, but the date of the main building has been put at about 1740 or earlier. There is a good staircase of this period and one room is panelled. To the west is the modern Baptist Church. On the other side of the street, No 63 has a picturesque front dated 1796 with a good doorway, and the attractive bay windows were added a few years later. The Conservative Club is mainly Late Georgian, and is now being extended on ground where once stood " The Pigeons ".

GREENHAM MILL

Part of Bone Lane Industrial Estate stands on the site of Greenham Mill. Greenham Mill House has been demolished in recent years. This was the scene of the making of the famous Throckmorton or Newbury Coat in 1811. *(see p. 51)*

STROUD GREEN

Beyond the ring road to the south-east is Stroud Green, a pleasant open space now owned by the Corporation.

Tudor Lodge

On the north side is Tudor Lodge, a fine three-storeyed house which appears to date from Queen Anne period, with a good staircase and front gate of that time. The lower east part of the house is partly timber-framed and possibly dates from the Jacobean period, with a very fine old fire place. Behind, and formerly part of this property, is a barn which has been converted into a charming residence. There are several small Mid or Late Georgian houses facing the Green to the east.

Thanks are due to all those who so kindly allowed their houses and buildings to be inspected for the compilation of this section of the book. The publishers will be most grateful for any additional information concerning buildings or their dates, and for any corrections, which may be incorporated in future editions.

Index

Abberbury, Sir Richard 25, 26
ABC Cinema 77
Adams 70
Albert Works 67
Anchor Inn, The 76-77
Andover Road 20, 39, 46, 82
Argyle Road 20, 24, 44, 46, 81
Armorial Bearings 12-13
Arts Centre 77

Bacon Arms, The 69
Baptist Church 90
Barclay's Bank 67
Bartholomew Close 81
Bartholomew Manor 81
Bartholomew Street 18, 20, 28, 45, 80, 88
Bath Road 20, 54, 67
Battle of Newbury, First 37, 86
Battle of Newbury, Second 40, 86
Beacon Hill 14
Bear Inn, The 69
Beynon's 82-83
Black Bear Lane 88
Black Boys, The 81
Blue Stockings 48
Bone Lane Industrial Estate 90
Borough of Newbury 11
Boys, Sir John 26, 40, 42, 43
Bread Riots 48
Bridge Street 77
Broadway, The 64, 68, 69, 70
Bronze Age 19
Burial Mounds 38, 40, 82

Camera Club 63
Camp Hopson's 76
Canals 47
Carnarvon, Fifth Earl of 14
Carnarvon, First Earl of 39
Carnegie Trust Fund 90
Castle Houses 67
Castle Inn, The 67
Castle, Newbury 22, 87
Cattle Market 56
Cemetery, New 82
Cemetery, Old 82
Chantry, The 79
Charles Lucas and Marshall 80
Charters 11, 23, 44
Charter Trustees 11
Cheap Street 18, 20, 60, 89-90
Chequers, The 69
Chestnuts, The 20, 68
Christ's Hospital School 45
Church Almshouses 82
City Recreation Ground 20, 61
Civil War 37
Clay Hill 41, 42, 46
Clock Tower 56
Cloth Hall 36, 62, 86
Cloth Trade 12, 29-36, 51, 86
Club House 79
Coach Trade 45-47, 54, 69, 70
Coat of Arms 11
Congregational Church 75
Conservative Club 90
Coopers 69
Cooper's Arms, The 80
Corke and Son, Wm. G. 76
Corn Exchange 56, 89
Coxedd, Francis 44, 45
Coxeter, John 51
Craven Road 80

Cromwell, Oliver 41-42
Cromwell Place 75
Cross Keys, The 70

Daniels' 88
Dark Ages 21
Davies 75
Day, Shergold and Herbert 84
Derby Road 20, 46
Dolman Family 35
Dolphin Inn, The 80
Domesday Survey 21
Donnington Castle 26, 40, 42, 43
Donnington Friary 25
Donnington Hospital 25

Eight Bells, The 80
Elizabeth Cottage 71
Essex, Earl of 37-40
Essex Street 39, 40, 82

Fair Close Day Centre 64, 82
Falkland Garth 39, 82
Falkland, Lord 39, 89
Falkland Memorial 39, 82
Freeman Hardy and Willis 76

Gaol, The 90
Garden House 81
George and Pelican, The 50, 53, 70
Globe Inn, The 44, 79
Golden Egg Restaurant 50, 76-77
Goldwell 68
Goldwell Park 61, 68
Grammar School (see under St. Bartholomew's)
Gramophone Society 63
Granary, The Old 86
Greenham Common 58, 61
Greenham House 61, 62
Greenham Mill 90
Greenham Mill House 90
Greenham Preceptory 23, 87
Griffin's 77
Guildhall 36
Guildhall Coffee House 83

Halifax Building Society, The 83
Hambridge Farm 73
Hambridge Frozen Foods 73
Hampton Road 46
Hamstead Park 14, 38
Hatchet Hotel, The 88
Hermitage Road 82
Hill Forts 20
Hilton 76
Hospital, Newbury and District 61, 82
Hymac Ltd. 68

Iron Age 19, 20

Jack of Newbury 12, 29, 34, 81
Jack of Newbury Inn, The 75
Jack of Newbury's House 31, 75
Jones and Sons, A. 75

Kendrick House 87
Kendrick's Charity 36, 45
Kennet and Avon Canal 47, 87
Kennet Bridge 29, 48-50, 77
Kennet River 9, 12, 47
Kennet Road 79, 89
Kimber's Almshouses 89
King Charles I 37-43
King Henry VIII 23, 24, 26, 31
King John 22, 24
King's Arms Inn, The 73
King's Coffee House 70
Kitchen and Bedroom Design 89

Lawrence's 75
Lemon Plaice, The 89
Library 62, 90
Literary Society 63
Litten Chapel 25, 29, 82
Lloyds Bank 70, 79
London Road 20, 68, 70, 73
Louch, Belcher and Co. 84

Machine Riots 53
Magistrates' Court 56, 64
Manchester, Earl of 40-42
Manfield's 75
Manor House 72
Mansion House Street 56, 82-83, 88

Market Place 18, 20, 29, 36, 48, 53, 60, 62, 83-84, 88
Market Street 89
Marks and Spencer 75
Marsh, The 31, 67, 77
Maynards' 75, 88
Mayor 11
Mesolithic Age 17
Michaelmas Fair 61
Millwaters 73
Milward's 76, 77
Money, Walter 18
Montagu, Mrs. 48, 61
Monument Inn, The 74
Municipal Buildings 56, 88
Museum 18, 20, 62, 86-87

Neate's 90
Neolithic Age 18
Newbury and District Field Club 18, 56, 63
Newbury and District Hospital 61, 82
Newbury Art Group 62
Newbury Arts Festival 63
Newbury Arts Workshop 63
Newbury Castle 22, 87
Newbury Coat 51, 86, 90
Newbury College of Further Education 61
Newbury District Council 11-13
Newbury Fine Art Group 63
Newbury Laundry 70
Newbury Martyrs 34
Newbury Music Festival 62
Newbury Skirmish 45
Newbury Station 55
Newbury Symphony Orchestra 62
Newbury Weekly News 62, 75
Newtown Road 20, 25, 44, 82
Northbrook Street 20, 28, 29, 31, 34, 48, 67, 73, 77
Northcroft 61, 63, 77
Northcroft Lane 28, 63, 77

Old King's Head Inn, The 88
Old Newtown Road 20, 46
Old Rectory 76-77
Old Waggon and Horses, The 84
Old Way, The 18
Olivers Shoes 75
Oxford Road 68
Oxford Street 20, 68-69

Paige's 75
Palaeolithic Age 17
Park House School 61, 82
Park Way 72, 77
Pearsons 70
Pelican Lane 68
Pembroke Road 28
Penn's 89
Phoenix, The 71
Pigeons, The 90
Pitman and Bazett 72
Plaza, The 88
Plenty's Lifeboat 53
Police Station 64
Porter, John 59
Post Office 89
Pound Street 19, 81
Presbyterians 45
Pyle Hill 20, 46

Quakers 44-45
Queen Elizabeth I 23, 26
Queen Elizabeth II 60
Queen's Hotel, The 80
Queen Victoria's Statue 61

Racecourse 51, 59
Railway 53-56
Rankin, John 86
Raymond's Almshouses 44, 81-82
Reading Co-op 80
Reformation 34
Ridgeway, The 18
Riviera, La 69
Rockingham 28
Roman Occupation 20
Rose and Crown Inn, The 76
Rupert, Prince 37, 38, 42

St. Bartholomew's Almshouses 58
St. Bartholomew's Grammar School 25, 28, 45, 60, 82
St. Bartholomew's Hospital 24

St. Gabriel's School 24, 61
St. George's Church 82
St. John's Church 58, 82
St. John's Infant School 82
St. Joseph's Church 73
St. Mary's Almshouses 90
St. Mary's Hill 90
St. Mary's Hospital 25
St. Nicolas' Church 21, 31-34, 58, 79
St. Nicolas' House 79
Salvation Army Hall 77
Sandham Memorial Chapel 14
Sandleford Hospital 61
Sandleford Link 64
Sandleford Priory 24, 48, 61
Sanger, George 61-62
Shaw 46
Shaw Bridge House 73
Shaw Crescent 19, 20, 73
Shaw House 34-36, 40-42, 86
Shaw House Comprehensive School 61
Shaw Mill 48
Shaw Road 20, 73
Skippon, General 38, 40, 41
Smallwood, John 29, 33
Smith and Sons, W.H. 48, 50, 77
Southern Electricity Board 68
Speen 20, 21, 41, 46
Speen Court 68
Speenhamland 19, 20, 46, 53, 56, 67, 69
Speenhamland Act 50
Speenhamland Lane 68
Speen Lane 20
Spencer, Stanley 14
Spring's Cafe 71
Stroud Green 46, 61, 90
Swimming Pool 63, 77

Tandoori Restaurant 75
Tea Bar 75
Temperance Hall 63, 77
Thatcham 20, 21, 40
Theatre, Old 69
Thresher's 88
Throckmorton Coat (see Newbury Coat)
Throckmorton, Sir John 51
Town Hall 56
Town Mill House 79
Tudor Lodge 91
Tumuli 19, 38, 40
Turnpike School 61
Turpin, Dick 73

Victoria Park 18, 19, 31, 61, 62, 67, 77
Vine, The 80
Vision Hire 74

War Memorial 57, 79
Wars of the Roses 23
Wash Common 10, 19, 61, 82
Waterside Chapel 45
Waterside Youth Centre 63
Weavers' Cottages 79
Welcome Cafe 89
West, John and Frances 45
West Mills 28, 79
West Mills Yard 79
West Street 75, 77
Wharf 22, 47, 86-87
Wharf Road 87
Wharf Street 84
Wharf Street Hall 84
White Hart Hotel, The 84
Winchcombe, John 29
Winchester College Hostelry 28
Woodhead's 70
Wood, John D. 72
Woolwich Equitable Building Society, The, 77
Woolworth's 75
World Wars 57

York House 70